MY TROPIC OF CANCER

···

LIVING & DYING WITH A DREAD DISEASE

D1606368

DANIEL MINTIE

Livingwell Publishing
Taos, New Mexico

Livingwell Publishing
1417 Santa Cruz Road
Taos, New Mexico 87571 USA
www.livingwellpublishing.com

Ordering Information:
Quantity sales. Special discounts are available on quantity purchases by corporations, associations, and others. For details, contact the "Special Sales Department" at the address above.

My Tropic of Cancer: Living & Dying With A Dread Disease, 1st edition
ISBN (Print Edition) 978-1-7328364-4-0
ISBN (Audiobook) 978-1-7328364-5-7
ISBN (Ebook) 978-1-7328364-3-3

Contents

For Nancy
Sister, co-conspirator, best friend

There is no old age, sickness or death. Also no ending of old age, sickness and death.

Prajñāpāramitāhṛdaya

<u>Origin</u>

After the final no there comes a yes
And on that yes the future world depends.
Wallace Stevens

I was born in spring, at the start of things. The year's final, wintry *no* was just giving way to a green and vernal *yes*. The sun was crossing the equator on its voyage north. The scale pans day and night hung suspended, dead level as the horizon twixt earth and sky. It was April first. It was Easter Sunday. Dr. Slater handed Mom her third-born, saying, "I don't know if this one is the Risen Lord or just some April Fool." I would have liked Dr. Slater. A wise guy like me. He was right, of course, on both counts. His being right is what this book is about: our divine and foolish voyage from birth to death. Another pair of scale pans, those two. Striking what balance they strike, as clocks strike and human hearts.

*

St. Luke's was a Catholic hospital. Mom and Dad were devout Catholics, which in part explains your reading this sentence. My parents didn't practice birth control. Mom would eventually have seven children, which put her in the middle of the pack in our Irish, working-class neighborhood. Mrs. Jones and Mrs. Donahue each had twelve. "Children are gifts from God," the Church taught. One had best not refuse divine gifts.

Nota bene: The magisterium, the teaching Church, was and is comprised of single men. While some are biological fathers, none are publicly so.

St. Luke's gave Mom and Dad a scrapbook published by the Catholic Manufacturing Company of New York, NY. *A Catholic Baby's Record* has pages in which parents paste things like birth and baptismal certificates, First Communion photos, and so forth. A sprawling tree is drawn across the first two pages. Titled *The Family,* the tree's branches have little scrolls printed with the words Father, Mother, Grandfather, etc. The Grandmother scroll on Mom's side has the name *Ruth* written in, and on Dad's side, the name *Irene.*

Two years to the month after my birth, Irene would die in a sanitarium 25 miles away. Her death certificate lists "Lymphosarcoma" as the cause of death. Lymphosarcoma is a cancer that arises in lymphocytes, immune cells that normally protect the body from threats. Such cells recognize the difference between us and not-us, then coordinate attacks on anything not-us: viruses, bacteria, cancer cells. Trojan-horse style, lymphosarcoma strikes at the heart of the body's defense system.

Bluntly put, it was Grandma Irene's own immune system that did her in.

*

Origin. From the Sanskrit *iyarti*: "to set in motion." I was set in motion one August night in the year preceding my birth. That night, one of Dad's spermatozoa hooked up with one of Mom's ova. As I would learn 17 years later in sophomore biology class, this blind date unleashed a torrent of activity in this earliest iteration of me. Over the next day and night, millions of distinct operations took place in that still-single cell's three billion base pairs of DNA. Proteins, enzymes, and epigenetic pointers got on their marks, got set. About 30 hours on, they would *go!* That first cell divided. Two cells became four became eight. I was on my way.

Had you known me then, during my first day and night on earth, you'd have called me *zygote*, a Greek word that means *yoke*. What was it getting yoked? Dad's sperm and Mom's egg were different from all other cell types in their bodies. Instead of having the usual 46 chromosomes, they each had 23. The missing 23 were supplied by the other party on that blind date, creating something without precedent in the history of the universe, something that would not again appear in any distant future: the particular set of proteins that would eventually write this record of those events.

Mom and Dad, of course, were set in motion just this way. And their moms and dads: Ruth's genes were in the mix that night, and Irene's. And so on, all the way back to the start of things.

*

Origin of species. What was that, and when? Humans weren't around, of course, though in a sense, we were. One could say we were around the corner. Looking back from that corner today, here's what we see:

Somewhere in the neighborhood of the Paleozoic in the superocean Panthalassa—an early ancestor of today's Pacific Ocean—two fat molecules merged into a larger entity called a micelle. Why they did this we don't know, but we do see such goings-on in laboratories today. We also see micelles again dividing, creating daughter micelles. Sounding familiar?

Floating, too, in that Paleozoic sea were strands of primordial RNA, glycosylamines that regularly linked themselves into chains. Then one such chain did something unprecedented: it copied itself. Why? Again, we don't know. Though, considering the 675 duodecillion (10^{39}) molecules on the planet at the time, the appearance of Earth's first self-replicating chemical was perhaps only a matter of time. And time is always an ingredient in any recipe.

Nota bene: While time is an essential ingredient, nobody has yet figured out exactly what time *is*. Unlike other phenomena like temperature, color, or sound, we have no "time receptors" in either our central or peripheral nervous systems. Some few of us have a sneaking suspicion that, for all the hullabaloo made about it, an entity known as time never has and never will exist at all outside the realm of human imagination.

*

Now. Some four billion years BCE, a particular micelle had a blind date with a particular self-replicating glycosylamine chain. We might call this divine union Earth's *ur-zygote*. Daughter cells carrying copies of the glycosylamine chain followed. And life on Earth was off to the races.

What races? Another one-off assembly of proteins would later name them "natural selection." Some matings of lipid and glycosylamine fared better than others. Time, existing or not, passed—some 3.5 billion years' worth of it. Then, 500 million years ago, the first vertebrates appeared in that sea. Some 300 million years later, the first mammals walked ashore. Primates showed up 75 million years ago, and hominids 55 million years after that. Homo sapiens, the race's most recent winners, crossed the finish line a mere 200 thousand years ago.

Homo sapiens, we self-described wise guys (at least we're honest about it). We'd beaten the rest of the Hominina subtribes across the finish line—though it would be more descriptive to say we're *just now* beating them. If that first blind date between micelle and glycosylamine occurred at the stroke of midnight on a 24-hour clock, wise guys would not appear for another 11 hours, 59 minutes, and 59 seconds.

Just now. What is that? A cognitive scientist might answer, "a functional brain state characterized by 30 milliseconds of neuronal oscillation." A philosopher might say, "a language game." And you? What would you say?

Nota bene: Time is short. You'd best answer now.

*

"At least we have our health," Mom says. It's a kind of mantra for her. I'm in third grade. My family is sitting together at our nine-seater kitchen table, discussing some deprivation or other, one or another misfortune that has befallen the Minties. We own one car, a three-bedroom house, and no spare change. Mom is the family barber and paramedic. Mom and Dad go out together to dinner without us once a year, on their wedding anniversary. On Mother's Day, all nine of us go to breakfast at the International House of Pancakes. All year I look forward to the blueberry pancakes.

We all came up in a world of hand-me-downs. Genes, first of all, but also jeans, and much else. Being third in the birth order, I got proportionally more first-hand stuff than my downstream sisters. I recently asked my sister Kathy what pre-owned items she remembered receiving. "I don't remember receiving anything *else*," she replied. "By Kid Number Five, it was pretty much all hand-me-downs, all the time. Clothes, shoes, bikes, lunch boxes, schoolbooks, toys, even my goddam bed." My youngest sister, Donna, adds to the list, "Roller skates, a violin, and tennis rackets. Also, Bermuda shorts, made from hot, sticky fabric that was super stretchy and never wore out."

We also handed down viruses, bacteria, the occasional fungus. Through 30 years of family pandemics, the Mintie children fell, domino-like. Each flu season, each outbreak of measles, mumps, or chickenpox. Except me. I was notoriously, maddeningly immune to every scourge that swept the house. My siblings had tonsils removed. Teeth filled, pulled, and straightened. I was an adult before having my first cavity. My one childhood concession to human frailty were the glasses I began wearing in third grade.

Over time, Mom's mantra went into me in a way I wouldn't notice until many years later. Parents say the darndest things, and these things have a way of shaping kids' belief systems about their world, their living and dying. Just below the level of awareness, I acquired my first belief about that condition we call health. The belief went something like this: *I don't need much of anything, so long as I have my health.*

Being the poster child for wellness, I was a good candidate for this belief. Health felt as omnipresent to me as the mostly clean air of my California childhood. I'd always had and always would have my health. On some preconscious level, I understood that lying in wait on the backside of this sunny formulation was another, darker construction: *You'd damn well **better** have your health! Lose **that** and you will be lost indeed.* Through the salad days of my boyhood, I understood in some dim way that I and everyone else was walking a tightrope. One misstep and we would, any one of us, be irrevocably lost.

Cancer sounded like the ultimate misstep—the disease, even the word itself, so terrible that its mention was avoided in polite company. During my boyhood, cancer patients worldwide were regularly not given their diagnosis. The disease was perceived by all parties to be so devastating that physicians believed sharing it would only hasten their patients' demise. Family members were instructed to keep the gravity of their loved one's condition to themselves.

Then, in 1964, Surgeon General Luther Terry released his advisory committee's report on *Smoking And Health*. The report's principal finding was a conclusive, causal link between this great American pastime and lung cancer. Himself a longtime smoker, Terry held his press conference on a Saturday, so as not to crash the stock market. Overnight, the C-word sprung up everywhere: at the top of the evening news, on the front page of *The New York Times*, on next month's cover of *The Saturday Evening Post*.

Thus the ultimate misstep arrived front and center in the national psyche. Yet even as we learned cancer was the second-leading cause of premature global death, a curious thing happened in my developing brain and body. I concluded I would never be a cancer patient. The C-word would apply to other people, not to me. All my short lifetime's health data suggested the ultimate misstep was one I would never make.

*

The mostly clean air of my California childhood. We'd drive through it on our way up the Central Valley to the Sierra Nevada for our annual mountain vacation, rolling down the station wagon windows for a better view of the biplanes spraying pesticide over the miles of row crops and orchards whose fruit we'd eat later that summer. I'd walk through it each weekday morning, with a couple of my sisters in their hand-me-down uniforms, to Our Lady of Perpetual Help School. The sisters of Notre Dame ran OLPH more or less along the lines Plato laid out for philosopher kings: *know what's right and make sure others do it.* First thing each morning, the sisters would have the entire student body stand, turn to the American flag in the front of our room, hold our right hands over our little hearts, and pledge allegiance. The pledge was, in other words, our first prayer of the day. It had all the elements of other prayers: a prescribed posture, a facing toward a symbol, a lilting cadence. In the primary grades at OLPH, none of us knew what *pledge* or *allegiance* meant. *Liberty and justice for all* sounded pretty good. The rest sounded like some kind of preamble.

By sixth grade, I knew what it meant to pledge allegiance and did so most earnestly every weekday morning. But I was no longer looking at the flag. I was looking at Laurie Schulte, who lived at the end of my block in another middling-sized Catholic family. To my 12-year-old eye, Laurie Schulte was God's cross between the Blessed Virgin Mary and Brigitte Bardot—with the best qualities of each. My deepest yearning was to walk home with Laurie after school and carry her schoolbooks. Carrying a girl's schoolbooks was widely recognized as being what the catechism called a sacrament: *an outward sign of an inner grace.* When our family moved away at the end of

8

my seventh-grade year, my deepest regret was never to have consummated my relationship with Laurie Schulte. Each afternoon she carried her own books, close to her bosom as girls did, standing tall, moving with the simple elegance of water, her blond hair shining in the mostly clean California air of my still mostly clean youth.

*

Allegiance dispensed with, we'd get on to our catechisms. The catechism was a grade-school compendium of Catholic theology. It posed such questions as (number 17): *Is Jesus God, or is He man, or is He both God and man?* Multiple-choice inquiries into the nature of ultimate reality. Some questions I've continued to ask myself to this day. Question 21: *What is your soul?* Question 39: *Who is your neighbor?*

Once each month, we'd hear the nearest air raid siren go off. The long, high-pitched wail was the sound we knew we'd hear when the Russians came to drop nuclear bombs on us. We were taught to *duck and cover*—get out of our seats and crouch beneath our desks, eyes closed and our hands over our heads. I remember kneeling there each month on the cold linoleum of Sister Saint John's classroom, eight-year-old eyes clenched, imagining the bomb going off on the basketball court outside, the bright light, the windows shattering. I remember asking my eight-year-old self this question: *Will this really save me?* Once the siren wound down, we'd get back into our seats and carry on with catechism. Question 55: *What is the sixth commandment?* Answer: *Thou shalt not kill.* Question 143: *What is hell?*

*

In seventh grade, I asked Gregory Wertz about one part of the pledge. Gregory Wertz was a fat kid who seemed dropped into OLPH from a Romanian gypsy camp. He played the accordion like Lawrence Welk and looked out on the world through the sad eyes of a grandfather. It was Gregory who one day explained to me what OLPH actually stood for: "Old Ladies Pool Hall." Hearing that, I took Gregory Wertz as my oracle and thenceforth consulted him in all things.

"Why do we say One Nation Under God?" I asked Gregory. His answer immediately clarified all manner of other things I'd been wondering about a good part of my first 13 years.

"People mostly call themselves stuff they're not," Gregory Wertz explained.

*

That first decade of my life were salad days for others than myself. The global traffic in all things nuclear went from being a well-hidden secret in the mountains near my present-day New Mexico home to the largest budget item in the history of the universe. Here are two notable events of this decade: 1] the world's first nuclear power plant went online in Obninsk, a town outside Moscow; 2] every other month, an above-ground nuclear test was conducted just over the state line in Nevada. The Atomic Energy Commission of One Nation Under God distributed radiation badges to our Silver State neighbors and urged them to sit outside on their decks to enjoy the mushroom clouds. Kind of like watching Fourth of July fireworks, I suppose. Though we Golden Staters couldn't enjoy that show, depending on which way the wind blew, we breathed in its radionuclides with the mostly clean air of my childhood.

Thirty years to the month following my birth, not far from Obninsk, the Chernobyl nuclear power plant melted down. This event released 400 times more radiation than the bomb One Nation Under God dropped on our Hiroshima neighbors. I was living in Heidelberg, Germany, at the time, less than a day's drive west. In the weeks that followed, everyone in Europe became, like the Silver State neighbors of my youth, *downwinders*. This time we weren't told to duck and cover. We were told to stay inside, consume no lettuce or milk, and wait. Listening to these instructions, we looked into each other's eyes and I recognized there the question I'd asked myself 22 years earlier beneath my desk in Sister Saint John's religion class.

*

Question 140: *What happens to men when they die?* Question 145 (the catechism's last): *In light of these truths, what should you do?*

<u>Sport</u>

It was when the trees were leafless first in November
And their blackness became apparent, that one first
Knew the eccentric to be the base of design.
Wallace Stevens

Earth is vagabond if she is anything. She pirouettes in a solar system itself in pivot round the center of its galaxy. This galaxy is hurtling through spacetime toward a nether region of the universe known as the Great Attractor. We don't know what the Great Attractor is, just that we're all heading there day and night at 600 kilometers per second.

Like her solar sisters, Earth circles the sun not in anything like goose step. From the sun's point of view, Earth sambas, swaying her hips like the girl from Ipanema on her way to the beach. It's this sashay through the star's warm gaze that gives Earth her seasons. And those seasons that bestow the gift of life in this shapely place.

Movement from some *here* to some *there* is the first principle. Atoms, quite like the planets made of them, are veritable whirling dervishes. Up and down any scale of spacetime, you'll find not a single thing not in a mad dash round.

*

The Persian poet Rumi established the Order of the Whirling Dervishes. He understood whirling as a way of syncing up with first principles: movement from here to there; this on its way to becoming that. Rumi may or may not have intuited our solar system's genesis story. It goes back 4.6 billion years to a whirling cloud of dust and gas gravity collapsed into a protostar that would become our sun. This infant sun was in turn encircled by another dusty whirligig that over millions of years coalesced into planetesimals that, when they grew up, became today's planets.

For any body—whirling or no—it's not so much that things change. It's just that there's no such thing as *staying put.*

*

The adult human body is an exquisite assemblage of 37 trillion cells, most all of which replace themselves every seven years. Lymphocytes live about a week. Ten percent of one's skeleton is swapped out annually. Human beings might better be called *human becomings.* Or better, human-comings-and-goings. Now *there's* the truth of us. Like the sun *en voyage* from tropic to tropic, like the earth stepping lightly through her seasons, wise guys are nothing if not underway.

And we've never traveled alone. Since *ur-zygote*'s appearance, all beings have advanced in each other's good graces. Advanced, in fact, *as* each other. So, too, each part of each other. Consider a single structure: the human tooth.

Our earliest vertebrate forebearers were shark-like fish cruising the Cambrian sea. These fellow travelers had no teeth, but their offspring developed scales with an outer dentin layer and vascular innards containing nerves and blood vessels. Over time, some such scales migrated into their mouths, creating the Cambrian prototype of today's great white shark. Modern great whites' scales and teeth are coded by the same proteins and grouped together in a single anatomical category called odontodes. Teeth conferred an evolutionary advantage, extracting more energy from food than had previously been available. So when vertebrates climbed out of the sea, they came bearing teeth. Nature, red now in tooth and claw, headed inland toward apples, beef jerky, and corn on the cob.

And it's not just teeth. Pick any structure in your body today and we can draw a clear, bright line back to critters cruising that Paleozoic sea. Hands? They come to us courtesy of *Elpistostege*, a tetrapod whose fins were the progenitors of our own limbs from the wrist down. They used these fins to hold themselves up in shallow water— much as we do—the better to breathe the air upon which all vertebrates thrive.

*

We ourselves—that is, all critters alive on the planet today—are the result of a dialectic. *Dialectic* is another word that comes to us from the Greek. Its Greek root translates as *conversation*. One conversant we could call *Way-Things-Are*, and the other *Hey-Guys-Watch-This!* Imagine that at some point this discourse had become a monologue. Were this to happen on the side of *Way-Things*, we might remain toothless, shark-like fish cruising a 21st-century sea. Were the monologue to occur on the side of *Hey-Guys!*, we'd be a random assortment of high-school chemistry experiments, none with the ways or means of apprehending ourselves or anything else.

This conversation continues moment to moment at the cellular level. On the *Way-Things* side, all those seven-year comings and goings are watched over from the start by an omniscience named the immune system. Like the God of my catechism (Question 12: *Does God know all things? Answer: Yes. Nothing can be hidden from God*), Omniscience keeps a stunningly close eye on cellular goings-on, right down to the molecular level.

Let's say Omniscience notices a brain cell releasing abnormal proteins. Left unchecked, those proteins can lead to the structural changes associated with Alzheimer's disease. Omniscience can respond to these beta-amyloids in a number of ways. It might, for instance, activate the ubiquitin-proteasome pathway, recycling the proteins into usable amino acids. Omniscience is like a security company, in diligent service to its principal client, *Way-Things.*

On the *Hey-Guys!* side, the genome is always rolling the dice, coloring outside the lines, running with scissors. *Hey-Guys!* is deeply subversive of established orders: toothless sharks, orderly lymphocytes, etc. *Hey-Guys!* is all about wild inventiveness. Some such wildings we're pretty happy about: the evolution of odontodes. Others we view as unmitigated personal and familial disasters: lymphosarcoma.

*

Nota bene: When speaking of abnormal proteins, we're describing a *statistical* circumstance: a numeric convention pointing to a rule. We're saying a particular condition hews toward or away from some norm. A disinterested, interplanetary observer might view the brain's development of beta-amyloids as being wholly normal. Might see the brain simply expressing another authentic aspect of itself, albeit a statistically anomalous one. As weather produces lightning strikes. As night sky falling stars.

Language is never value-neutral. When I learned in Sister Mary Saint Dorothy's second-grade classroom that a certain crayon in my Crayola set was named *flesh*, I didn't notice until years later what else I learned. Just so, the word *abnormal* was, from the start, inflected with ethical and moral overtones. It traveled in such company as *abnormous* and *monstrous*. Mel Brooks famously employed this trope in his movie *Young Frankenstein*. Dr. Frankenstein asks his lab assistant Igor for the name on the jar from which came the brain the doctor transplanted into his increasingly disturbed creature.

"Abby," Igor says, smiling sweetly.

"Abby—who?" asks the doctor, a terrible light coming into his face.

"Abby Normal," Igor replies proudly.

And we all know how *that* experiment turned out.

*

Gregor Mendel was the first scientist to listen in on the conversation between *Way-Things* and *Hey-Guys!* He did this while sitting in a pea patch. Mapping how physical characteristics (phenotypes) were transmitted from one pea generation to the next by means of genes (genotypes), Mendel noticed random mutations occurring. He called these mutations "sports." *Hey-Guys!*—a sporting fellow through and through—would relish this term. As chromosomal replication marched on its orderly way, *Hey-Guys!* would occasionally show up and slip unnoticed into the parade. This new band member would then get encoded into the genotype going forward, expressing itself in the new phenotype.

And the band played on its ever-so-slightly different tune.

*

The key word in the last paragraph is *unnoticed*. Slips that Omniscience notices are dealt with as harshly as God's enemies in the Hebrew Bible. In order to survive, *Hey-Guys!* has developed hundreds of strategies to do what my schoolboy self sometimes wondered if I might do: evade God's implacable view, if only for a moment. Here's one such strategy:

Our 37 trillion cells, going about their daily business of orderly replacement, listen in on each other. They listen by means of *growth factors*, proteins present in all human tissue. While growth factors are relatively few and far between, they produce an outsize effect. These proteins essentially control all cellular activities, including a cell's orderly birth, specialized life, and timely death. Growth factors are like neighborhood gossip: any one cell has the scoop on any other in its particular 'hood, also known as its microenvironment. This one-for-all, all-for-one approach is hugely protective of all parties. Like a good neighborhood block watch program, it ensures the wellness of each resident and of their neighborhood as a whole. Bad guys (in our telling, *Hey-Guys!*) had best beware. Suspicious activity will immediately be reported to the authorities. A swift, armed response is promised to follow.

Given *Way-Thing*'s neighborhood watch and many other security operations, what's a *Hey-Guys!* to do? Particularly if its agenda is the development of a (note the anything-but-neutral tone) malignant tumor.

For starters, *Hey-Guys!* might tinker with growth factors themselves, creating the equivalent of its own neighborhood watch. Most growth factors are synthesized in one type of cell and designed to act on a different cell type. Cancer evolved a new trick: the ability to synthesize growth factors that act on a cancer's *own* cell types. As these cancer cells divide, their daughter cells promulgate this new growth factor, enabling unlimited cellular division at that site. A tumor is now free to grow beneath the radar of the neighborhood block watch.

Cancer might also take a different approach. Leaving growth factors alone, it can dramatically increase the number of *receptors* for them on the surfaces of cancer cells. While the quantity of growth factor in the cellular neighborhood remains the same, cancer cells' responsiveness to it is massively increased. Ambient levels of growth factor that typically would not initiate cellular division now does so in spades.

Wildly inventive, running with scissors through the cellular neighborhood, cancer has many other tricks up its sleeve. Growth factor receptors are like old-fashioned light switches. They have but two positions, off and on. Cancer is able to selectively snip out the regulatory segments of receptors, leaving them permanently in their *on* position. Uncontrolled growth has ruined many human places. Observers have remarked on the similarity between aerial photos of urban areas blighted by overdevelopment and electron microscope images of carcinomas.

In the following chapter, we'll look at some essential links between these two environs.

Neighborhood

My window is twenty-nine three
And plenty of window for me.
Wallace Stevens

*H**ey-Guys!* has from the start been staunchly holding up its side of the conversation, that dialectic that is life on Earth. Without *Hey-Guys!* there'd simply be no *ur-zygote*, no earthly life. The fixity we perceive as that life, in individuals or in species, is an optical illusion. It's the fixity we perceive in a mountain, in anything at all. Such perception stops the action, halts the mad dash round, as does a photograph (though photos, too, are on their own mad dash). *Way-Things* appears as bubbles on the surface of the sea. *Hey-Guys!* gives birth to each bubble and returns it to its source.

When *Hey-Guys!* appears as one of 100 types of human cancer, it can be the result of a simple cellular dice roll. These are the appearances Mendel called *sports*. There's nothing more involved here than the craps game that is the human genome. With six billion base pairs of DNA in every cell, some chromosomal slippage during a particular cell division will inevitably occur. What's astonishing is the rarity of these occurrences. Though they increase with age, they account for a very small fraction of cancers in the world today. What accounts for the rest?

Genes, for one. Irene passed her genes to Dad, and Dad passed them to me. In families with cancer histories, cellular dice get preloaded. Ten percent of melanomas and breast cancers and up to 60% of endometrial cancers can be traced to inherited genes. Certain genes convey increased risk of multiple cancers: the BRCA mutation drives significantly greater risks of both breast and ovarian cancer. Another common mutation appears to drive both colorectal and lung cancers. A gene's *penetrance*— that is, its likelihood of being expressed in a particular family—has a lot to do with whether it will lead to the development of a cancer or not.

Then there are viruses, both the DNA and RNA varieties. Viruses account for up to 15% of cancers worldwide. These include the Epstein-Barr, hepatitis B, and herpes viruses. Versions of the human papillomavirus (HPV), after infecting squamous cells in the cervix, throat, and mouth, can drive genetic changes that result in carcinomas. HPV is the cause of nearly all cervical cancers, 90% of anal cancers, and 75% of vaginal cancers.

So: let's do the numbers. *Sports*, genes, and viruses together account for about 20% of the global cancer burden. What's missing from this picture?

We might call what's missing the elephant in the room. So far we've been looking at cancer's microenvironment: goings-on in the cellular neighborhood which, left unchecked, can produce malignant tumors. Yet 80% of world cancer risk is *not* driven by this intimate neighborhood. It's about another, much larger neighborhood that every human being lives in as well. We could call this neighborhood cancer's *macroenvironment*. Let's visit two such neighborhoods.

*

Any macroenvironment has two dimensions: a particular place and a particular time. A unique point in spacetime is the setting for all activity in the universe. And while space and time purport to describe separate things, they are in fact lenses through which we perceive a single reality. Apart from space, there is not time. Apart from time, no place. The same network of cells in the human hippocampal-entorhinal system tracks movement through both dimensions.

The Dakhla Oasis during the Ptolemaic dynasty was one such spacetime address. The oasis lies in central Egypt just above Tropic of Cancer. The Ptolemy family was the longest and last Egyptian dynasty, established in 305 BCE by Ptolemy I and ending in 30 BCE with the death of Cleopatra. What was it like to live and die in this neighborhood?

The oasis was an agricultural society. Neighbors lived in adobe brick homes and raised the cereal crops, dates, chick peas, lentils, and leeks that are staples of the modern Egyptian diet. While they ate fish, they consumed little red meat. They were physically active—farmers, craftspeople, builders of the enormous stone monuments still standing today. Their water and air were quite clean. While they inhaled a bit of cooking fire smoke and incense in their temples, looking up at night they clearly saw the *Heavenly Nile* draped overhead. The Romans would later call this view into the center of the galaxy the *Milky Way*. In the oasis, it was a view associated with Hathor, a goddess who bestowed wellbeing and abundance on all.

Hathor seems to have been on the job in this neighborhood. Life there appears to have been very good.

How about death? Modern paleopathologists have examined mummies from the oasis to determine causes of premature death. Most of these deaths were due to microbial diseases such as malaria and tuberculosis. Pathogenic fungal infections and caries killed a few oasis dwellers before their time. Cancer is startlingly absent—in either human or non-human oasis tissue preserved from that time. Its very occasional appearance was likely of the *sport* variety. The vast, well-preserved literature of the Ptolemaic era makes virtually no mention at all of any disease process resembling cancer.

*

Another neighborhood: London at the turn of the 19th century. With the Industrial Revolution in full swing, England was transitioning from an agricultural society reminiscent of the oasis to the manufacturing giant it is today. Human-made chemicals entered both the production stream and the nation's physical streams, rivers, and groundwater. Handwork was being replaced by machines. Steam powered those machines and burning coal created the steam. By the end of the 19th century, London had acquired a new moniker: *The Big Smoke*. Were there a *Heavenly Thames* flowing overhead, few Londoners saw it. Such was life at this spacetime address. How about death?

The 16th-century Swiss physician Paracelsus had noted a new lung disease killing metal miners in Saxony and Bohemia. He named it *Mala Metallorum*, suspecting a link between the illness and occupational exposure in the mines. Later researchers would identify this *metal malady* as a form of lung cancer, caused by the inhalation of radioactive dust associated with the mining of these metals. (Three hundred years and half a world away, Diné [Navajo] uranium miners in the American Southwest would succumb to the same disease—known now as *pulmonary neoplasm*—at 400 times the rate of non-mining members of the Navajo Nation.)

As industrialization swept Europe, other scientists began tying exposure to chimney soot, machine oils, industrial dyes, and many other new chemicals to the emergence of a plethora of mysterious, deadly, and as yet unnamed disorders. In hindsight, the Industrial Revolution can be seen as a global timestamp for the explosion in the rate of virtually all cancers seen today—and for cancer's emergence as the second leading cause of global death. We can trace a direct correlation between the number and quantity of 200 known and suspected carcinogens entering the air, water, and food of the world's neighborhoods and the incidence of the cancers they produce.

In the developing world today, this historical phenomenon is being recreated in real time. Over the last 30 years, Nigeria has experienced its own version of the Industrial Revolution and the cascade of mutagenic chemicals that flow from it. The incidence of breast cancer in Nigerian women has significantly increased over this period, tracking the rise of manufacturing. Rising levels of lead and other industrial metals in Nigeria's neighborhoods has been directly tied to these cancers. Laboratory studies find lead exposure produces mammary tumors in female mice and weakens their immune system's response to these tumors. Widescale copper mining in northern Chile in the 1950s led to arsenic levels in drinking water 17 times higher than those deemed safe by the World Health Organization. Arsenic exposure is a known risk factor for bladder cancer, and bladder cancer rates in that part of the country rose 400% as a result.

In many other Third World neighborhoods, increasingly polluted air has been tied to rising rates of the epigenetic changes that drive lung and other cancers, as well as a host of neurodegenerative diseases. One such disorder, Alzheimer's disease, is now being diagnosed in these neighborhoods in people in their 30s—decades before the disease typically emerges. All these tissue changes have been found in the brains and bodies of infants and children under the age of one. In One Nation today, 200 million pounds of arsenic-laced chemicals are fed to chickens each year.

*

Millennia of data now make clear that cancer's skyrocketing incidence, like the rate of modern climate change, is overwhelmingly a result of human activity. Seen in this light, cancer is less the problem than a symptom of the problem. Cancer is the body's protest against a neighborhood that, for the last two centuries, has become increasingly hostile to every life form. It is our humanness crying out for help.

<u>Tropic</u>

Now in midsummer come and all fools slaughtered
And spring's infuriations over and a long way
To the first autumnal inhalations, young broods
Are in the grass, the roses are heavy with a weight
Of fragrance and the mind lays by its trouble.
                                        Wallace Stevens

I rise before sunup each summer solstice, go outside, and wait. For what? Listen: a lone cricket's metallic bleat rising with the dew off the new grasses. A Steller's jay's rapid-fire *chook chook chook chook* racketing through the fir trees like a cold car engine trying to turn over. I inhale deep lungfuls of the exhalation of those fir branches, of the Rocky Mountain irises' lilac carpet on the high meadow at my feet. The eastern sky brightens to the hue of the iris petals, the forest greens emerge from the forest shadows. As the visual world steps forward, the sound of the river behind me recedes, playing more softly now, *piano* in its stone bed.

First sunlight bursts over the ridge. The warmth of my body rises through the cool, dry air to meet the star's

27

warmth. A homecoming of sorts. A kiss. The star's long gift of 9900 °F bestowing the gift of my body's 98 °F. I close my eyes and drink in this kiss, seeing blood red through my eyelids. A kiss intimate as any kiss. Interstellar. Real, as too few things in my life are real. This is not opinion, received wisdom, any argument for or against. This is reality itself, one point on the lengthening arc of my living-cum-dying.

For this I rise before sunup on the longest day.

*

Summer solstice, like the rest of life, is a local event. It never exists in the abstract. This year it occurs for me near my home in the United States' Rocky Mountains. More specifically, in the Pecos Wilderness, a protected area of 12,000-foot peaks with snow lingering still on their north-facing moraines. Cutthroat trout ply its streams. Bear and elk walk its woods. Human artifacts found here date back 9,000 years. Wise guys have been spending solstices in the Pecos for a while now. My wife and I are camping here, having backpacked in two days before.

At noon, 1,300 miles south of here, 23.43651 degrees north of the equator, the sun will stand directly overhead. If its rays were plumb lines, they would fall perpendicular to the planet's surface at that exact latitude. The latitude itself was named Tropic of Cancer at the start of the Common Era. The word *tropic* comes from the Greek word *trope*, which in English denotes a *change of direction* or *change in circumstance*. Astronomically, this change today is the sun's starting its return trip south. In six months, it will arrive 23.43651 degrees *south* of the equator, a latitude known as the Tropic of Capricorn.

Nota bene: While the June sun lay in the constellation Cancer at the start of the Common Era, it has since moved into the constellation Taurus. This astronomic slip-page, known as the precession of the equinoxes, gives the lie to notions about heaven's fixity. Even in heaven, *Hey-Guys!* has a hand in.

The constellation we call Cancer has long been named for critters with exoskeletons. In the Dakhla Oasis it was called Scarab, for a beetle associated with immor-tality that played a prominent role in the Middle King-dom's funerary rites. The Romans named it Cancer, after the crustacean whose shape it brought to the Latin mind. The Western physicians Hippocrates and Galen appropri-ated the word to name a swelling very occasionally ob-served in human tissue, a growth that hijacks the body's endothelial cells, creating new blood vessels to supply a tumor's growth. The shape these vessels create reminded these first doctors of the crustacean then and now scuttling across Aegean tide pools, a figure also seen making its seasonal way across the night skies.

*

The cutthroat in the Pecos streams is named for its bright crimson gill patches. It looks as though it's just swum through the hands of Jack the Ripper. When it comes to animals, nature is parsimonious in her use of this color. It dabs the crop of the ruby-throated hummingbirds that ap-pear at our feeders each spring. It wraps like a mask the eyes of sandhill cranes now hatching their colts 2,500 miles north near the Arctic Circle. It seems nature prefers this pigment *inside* its creatures, not outside. *Erythro-phobia*—fear of the color red—is likely one result. So too *hemophobia*, fear of the sight of blood. Globally, emer-gency vehicle and automobile brake lights are always red, in line with the 1949 Geneva Convention on Road Traffic. With the longest wavelength of any color, red light passes more quickly through glass than any of its fellow travelers. More red Ferraris leave the factory in Maranello than any other color. If urgency had a natural hue, it would be red.

I walk over to a fir tree to pee. I don't know why guys, both the four- and two-legged persuasions, most want to pee *on* something. Some universal tendency passed down from father to son in the shape of that Y chromosome. Something about territory, about competition. Looking down, I see something I've never seen before: a *change in circumstance.* I can't know it yet, but what I'm seeing will forever reset the arc of my living-cum-dying.

My pee is streaked with red bright as a cutthroat's gills.

*

Over the next weeks, the red tide ebbs and flows. *Hematuria* it's called, and it can be a symptom of many things: infection, traumatic injury, kidney stones, even strenuous exercise. Men over 50 with enlarged prostates can experience occasional hematuria. Pee can also flow red after eating beets, in which case it's called—I kid you not—*beeturia.*

There's no pain associated with my condition, whatever it might be. I think mostly about other things. I'm a busy guy, and my current stretch of road is busier than usual. Days in a row pass in which what emerges from my *meatus,* that bottommost passageway between myself and the world, looks entirely normal. Then the tide again flows red. I finally get in to see Alan, my family doctor, who collects a urine sample and concludes I likely have a low-grade urinary tract infection. I do a ten-day course of antibiotics, which seems to clear everything up.

Until it doesn't. I return and ask for a second, different course of antibiotics. My doctor considers this for a moment, then agrees. I'm the extraordinarily healthy guy I've always been. Urinary tract infections have adapted (*Hey-Guys!*) to the drugs used against them, becoming increasingly treatment resistant. It's late July. We'll give the new drug a couple of weeks and see what happens. On my way out of the exam room, I pass Alan in the hallway.

"Hey doc, we can rule out cancer as any kind of factor, right?"

Alan looks me in the eye and answers in a dead-level tone, "No, Daniel. We absolutely *cannot* rule out cancer."

*

Late August. My neighborhood is heading toward its own fall equinox. Soon the scale pans *day* and *night* will again strike their perfect balance at the horizon's beam. The days remain warm, but the nights bring our first autumnal inhalations: pinion smoke, roasting green chili, dry wheat and buffalo grasses. Yellow returns to the cottonwood trees. The last hummingbirds leave our feeders and head down to their winter range in Mexico. Soon the sandhill cranes and their spring colts will reappear overhead, creaking and croaking en route to their winter home at the bosque 100 miles south. They've been making the journey for 2.5 million years, their voices far older than any other in the sky. Higher still Aries, the zodiac's first constellation, will reappear in the night skies. I was born under this sign. My natal chart informs me, "The body comes first with Aries people. Natural athletes, they're not big on planning ahead. What's happening in the moment is what's most important to Aries."

What's happening in the moment: I'm prone on an exam table in a urologist's office in Albuquerque. The red tide kept returning and Alan referred me to the guy standing between my knees at the foot of the table. My feet are propped in stirrups, and I'm about to experience a procedure called cystoscopy. As soon as Alan said the word, I disliked it. The more I learned about the procedure, the more I disliked it. I lost sleep thinking about the cystoscopy in the weeks before this appointment. Cystoscopy starts with the introduction of a light and camera into the meatus, that orifice through which pee exits my body. So far as I'm concerned, things are already off to a bad start. All my life, the direction of travel has been *down* this passageway, the routing for which the male urogenital system is designed. An upstream journey seems as ill-advised as driving the wrong way up a one-way street. In the dark.

After insertion, the cystoscope will be pushed upward the length of my urethra, through the middle of my prostate, past my ejaculatory duct and urethral sphincter, arriving finally inside my bladder. There it will allow the urologist to examine that organ's innards. The procedure is performed under general anesthesia in hospitals. It's also performed, after sedation, in a doctor's office, like most colonoscopies. In my case, it's simply being performed.

"We don't use any anesthesia or sedation," the urologist tells me when I inquire.

"How come?" I ask.

"Insurance doesn't cover it," he replies.

Six walls away, sitting in the waiting room, my wife Julie's heart stops hearing me scream. Leaving the office, I tell her, "I feel like I've just been raped."

*

Having had his way with me, the urologist says he found a tumor near where my urethra enters my bladder. It looks like a cancer known as *papillary urothelial carcinoma*. It's about three inches in diameter. Its sloughing off cells is what's been causing the hematuria. He recommends surgery to remove it. He says until the tumor has been cut out and sent to pathology we won't know its grade or stage. His next opening for such a surgery is six weeks away. I take it on the spot.

Julie drives me home. I mostly sit in dazed silence. My entire life, it's been *other* people who've gotten cancer. The urologist said he couldn't be absolutely certain about his diagnosis: there is a one percent chance the growth isn't malignant. Only pathology could confirm things. Somehow, riding home, this one percent seems the larger number.

"It's probably all some big mistake," I tell Julie.

Tears in her eyes, she reaches across the console and takes my hand.

*

Cancers, like schoolchildren, get sorted into *grades*. A grade one cancer is the metabolic equivalent of a school's primary grades. Under a pathologist's microscope, these cancers more closely resemble normal tissue than do the upper grades. Their growth rate, too, is closer to that of healthy cells. As a result, they are described as *less aggressive* and perceived as a less imminent threat to their hosts. As cancers move through middle school toward high school, their cell structure appears increasingly abnormal and their growth rates increase. These characteristics make grade-four cancers, the highest grade, increasingly lethal and call for more immediate and aggressive intervention.

Cancers are also ranked by *stage*. Stage essentially refers to the age of a tumor. How long it has existed, how large it is, to what extent it has gone beyond its primary site and spread to other locations. Stage is also rated on a scale from one to four. A stage one cancer is relatively new and confined to a single tissue neighborhood. A stage four cancer has been around long enough to *metastasize*—that is, spread beyond its initial site, perhaps to a distant organ. The word comes from the Greek *methistanai*, a rhetorical term describing a sudden transition in subject matter. It first entered medical use in English during the Industrial Revolution. Today metastases account for 90% of all cancer deaths.

I do some quick math. My carcinoma must have been with me awhile to grow three inches across. It's certainly been around well before I began seeing blood in my urine eight weeks ago. In another six weeks, it might well be a year old. As with a schoolchild, the older a tumor, the higher its grade. Higher, too, the chance it will have grown through the inner lining of the bladder into the muscle that forms the outer wall of the organ. As muscle is vascular tissue, cancer cells there could migrate and reseed themselves anywhere my blood flows. As the days tick by, I often wonder exactly how that process might be progressing inside me. On what day—has that day come and gone? —will cancer leave my bladder and hit the road? Common bladder cancers cross the blood-brain barrier, leaving the patient, per the National Library of Medicine, "with an ominous diagnosis."

I call the surgeon's office, give the receptionist my mobile number, and tell her if someone cancels a surgery appointment I'll take it. No notice required. I'll be at the hospital in two hours.

*

The office doesn't call. Days stretch into weeks. The weather keeps cooling, the equinox comes and goes. Two great horned owls move down from the spruce-aspen zone and take up residence on the high mesa that is also my home. The male sits atop our stovepipe in the early morning hours. Amplified by the metal tube, we feel his deep *woof woof woof* reverberating in our chests. Some mornings I wake forgetting my medical status. These moments the world looks and sounds and smells much the way it always has in early fall. Construction paper cutouts of orange jack-o'-lanterns and black witches appear on the windows of the elementary school. Election signs spread through the neighborhood like seeds of the late grasses. The archaic cries of the cranes pass south in flights throughout the shortening days.

Then I remember: *I likely have cancer.* Surgery is scheduled for the first Friday in October. I'll go in two days before for bloodwork and an EEG. I'll talk to the anesthesiologist, receive post-op instructions and a prescription for pain pills. A medical student will ask me to sign a form permitting tissue they remove from me to be sent to a bank of such specimens available to researchers.

Such moments of remembering foreshorten my life in a new and curious way. I've always perceived *the future* as an amorphous, open field, much like the one we look through to the horizon—knowing, as we look, that while we can move *toward* that imaginary line, we'll never reach it. There is no edge out there over which ships or human beings could fall and be seen no more.

Except now there is. On or about that first Friday next month, I will receive new information about my future. In our last conversation, the word *mortality* slipped from my oncologist's lips. The word was directed at me. I found myself for the first time in a cohort referenced in the university hospital's grand rounds when I was in graduate school. Grand rounds are plenary sessions, open to physicians, residents, and students, in which a provider presents a particular patient's course of treatment and its outcome. Those sessions frequently took the form of *M&M conferences*—presentations on morbidity and mortality. Blunt, unsentimental statements of disease and death. Sitting in the plush, theater-style chair in the big auditorium, morbidity and mortality seemed entirely *over there*, up on stage, a spectacle as proximate to me as a distant spiral nebula were that the content of the presentation.

*

Julie is suffering more than me. I'll glance across the room and through the thinning afternoon sunlight see her looking at me with tears in her eyes. My heart starts breaking and I feel tears come to my eyes. We hug each other a lot. Sit in our summer shorts on the couch, bare legs touching. In the mornings Julie sits before her altar, chanting the healing meditation *Ra Ma Da Sa*. She learned it from her yoga teacher, teaches it to her own students, and is now chanting it for me. The syllables are Sanskrit words, each its own mantra. They translate as *Sun Moon Earth Infinity*—another formulation of living-cum-dying. Her voice is deep and strong, issuing from the same primal source as the owl's, reverberating through the morning house, reminding me I'm home.

I, too, am suffering, of course. Not so much physically: one of cancer's lethal stealth mechanisms is its early painlessness I do understand a bit more the fatigue I've felt these last months.

"Of course you're tired," Julie says. "In addition to everything else you're up to, your immune system has been doing some heavy lifting."

Most of my suffering is emotional. I worry about how far advanced the cancer might be. About how the surgery will go. About how Julie will do with things. About complications from surgery and the pain I might feel afterward. In short, about what the surgeon might find when he starts downcutting and what those findings will mean for us. Male metastatic bladder cancer, even if it remains localized to the urogenital tract, often calls for removal of the bladder, prostate, and other soft parts. Parts to which, we could say, I'm rather attached.

My wheelchair-bound high school chemistry teacher, Mr. Quinn, wore a bag into which pee drained. As the day went on, you could see it swell there beneath his belt. Along with his wheelchair, his chemistry lab blackboard lowered so that he could reach it from his chair, that bag located Mr. Quinn as the unlucky *other*, the one different from me. Different from *us*: the *normal* ones. *Other* as was the young boy my age at church each Sunday, strapped into his wheelchair so his spasms didn't throw him to the floor. Not making conscious connections to such as him, we normal ones would demean each other on the playground with the word *spaz*. The word *retard*. Or, on the boys' side of the playground, the word *woman*.

*

Though Mr. Quinn was *other*, I noticed he was also just like me: a wise guy. One day, instead of chemistry, we were talking about women's liberation. Charles Frisco told the class that, the Catholic church aside, women could no longer be excluded from membership in civic organizations or public places.

"The place me and my friends hang out *always* excludes women," Mr. Quinn said.

"No way!" Charles Frisco exclaimed. "That's illegal. Where do you guys hang out?"

"The men's room," Mr. Quinn replied.

*

Apart from those first forgetful moments of the day, I live in a state of low-grade anxiety. As a cognitive-behavioral therapist, I regularly measure the intensity of my patients' feelings. Measuring the daily intensity of my own anxiety, I find it averaging about 30%. Not disabling: I continue to do what I do. And I don't much see anything to be done to reduce or eliminate this emotion. It seems to come with the territory for any new cancer patient in the weeks leading up to organ cancer surgery. If this is so, I'm willing to accept it.

Then, one day, I discover I've *not* accepted it. At some subconscious level, I've been casting about for a new position in these facts that will relieve me of anxiety, perhaps replace it with some new emotion. Here's how I found out:

I'm riding my mountain bike pretty damn quickly down the hill above the plaza. Afternoon sunlight sparkles in the cottonwood branches, turning them stained-glass gold. I'm focused on the roadway directly in front of me, the potholes and patches of gravel in the curves. As prairie dogs, rabbits, snakes, and the occasional coyote often use our local roads, I'm keeping half an eye out for them as well. I'm not thinking about cancer. Not thinking about anything. I'm just riding my living-cum-dying down through the golden light when a single blessed thought comes to me.

Such blessing occurs maybe once or twice a month. Out of the usual white noise in my head steps an idea so simple, so elegant, it changes everything. Today's thought: "I could call the local cancer treatment centers and offer psychotherapy to newly diagnosed patients like myself. New fellow travelers feeling anxiety or panic or despair."

Coincident with the arising of this thought, two other things happen. One, I realize that when I arrive home I'll make those calls. Two, for the first time since my own diagnosis, my anxiety drops to zero. In its place rush in feelings of confidence, excitement, gratitude. And a surprising, deep, and abiding peace.

Handiwork

Ah, but to play man number one,
To drive the dagger in his heart,

To lay his brain upon the board
And pick the acrid colors out...
Wallace Stevens

I'm sitting across from Julie and our pal Michael at the hospital cafeteria table, watching them eat breakfast. They're eating apologetically, as I've been forbidden food and drink, water included, in advance of my 11:00 a.m. surgery. General anesthesia relaxes gastrointestinal muscles that prevent the stomach's contents from backing up into the lungs. I've eaten nothing since a light meal yesterday evening that I named *The Last Supper*. Julie found this unfunny.

We were up at dawn. I showered with the antiseptic wash I got at my appointment yesterday, and we drove to the hospital through morning traffic. Like an international flight, they tell you to come hours ahead of the actual surgery time. Now, checked in, plastic name bracelet on my wrist—*in case I forget who I am,* I tell Michael—there's nothing for us to do but wait. Michael and I go outside to a small enclosed garden and do some tai chi. The sun feels good on my skin. The movement brings me back out of my thoughts and into my body. A pretty good place to be most days, including this one. So far, anyway.

I'll be undergoing a surgery called *transurethral resection of the bladder.* The unwieldy name is a reasonable fit for what, when described, sounds like an unwieldy procedure. For starters, the light and camera crew will travel back up the same route they took during my cystoscopy. This time, the crew will also be packing the medical equivalents of a switchblade and a blowtorch. Arriving inside my bladder, the surgeon—observing his work on a color monitor above the cutting board—will slice out the tumor, then cauterize the wound to inhibit bleeding and give the bladder a jump start on healing itself. He'll make a point of *getting clean margins,* cutting beneath the cancer into healthy tissue so the pathologist can confirm the extent of its spread. Then he'll infuse a chemotherapy drug into my bladder that will, hopefully, kill any cancer cells released in the mayhem, preventing their reseeding new tumors.

I return to the registration desk at 10:00 and am told my surgery has been set back. When I return at 11:00, it's been again set back. I'm getting hungry. Antsy. I'm leaned over a stream at the water fountain before I remember, lick my dry lips, and walk away. At noon the clerk says they're ready for me in pre-op, and I say goodbye to Julie and Michael. They'll be allowed in to see me again once I'm prepped. The surgery will last an hour or so and we'll all go home in the late afternoon. I hold this image in mind: released from the stacked stories of crowded green hallways, their antiseptic atmosphere, their overly

loud PA announcements, back into the sunlight and bird-
song and late leaves where I belong.

I get undressed, put my clothes and shoes in a plastic bag, and don my green gown. One nurse starts an IV
while another checks my vitals and attaches electrodes to
my chest. A third asks me lots of questions, including
when I've last eaten, why I'm here today, if I have any
implants, and writes my answers down on her clipboard.
The anesthesiologist stops by and tells me about the cock-
tail of drugs he'll be using, about the tube he'll insert into
my airway once I'm under. He says he'll be beside me
during the entire procedure, a statement I find strangely
comforting. Lying here among strangers, as helpless as I
remember ever feeling, shivering from the cold, the im-
pending surgery, my falling blood sugar, any words I
might construe as kind are immensely welcome.

Prep finished, the crew moves on to the next station and Julie and Michael come in. In their eyes I see the
love and concern they'd each find in mine were our places
switched. Julie sits beside me, takes my hand, asks about
the lines and wires leading from my body to the apparatus
overhead.

"Your hand's so *cold*!" she says, rubbing it between hers. Michael gets a blanket from the nursing station and drapes it over me. Now the crew again descends
on me and, for the first time today, things start moving
quickly. Julie kisses me, tells me she loves me, and Michael does the same. As they're ushered to the waiting
room, a nurse takes Julie's cell number and says she'll text
her updates. Julie turns at the door, tears in her eyes, and
blows me a kiss. I blow one back, glad she'll not be sitting
by herself for the next hours.

I'm wheeled on the gurney out of pre-op, down a
series of long hallways crowded with staff and other gur-
neys. Mostly I have views of the dropped ceilings, the

fluorescent lights. Someone wipes a card through a slot and I'm pushed through double doors into the operating room, a large space with more people in it than I'd imagined finding. I'm transferred to the operating table and connected to more wires and tubes. The surgeon's face floats into view and asks if I have any questions. I can't at this point imagine a single one. The anesthesiologist places a plastic mask on my nose and mouth, says I'll feel tingly, and tells me to count backward from ten.

My whole body starts buzzing lightly. *Ten. Nine. Eight. Seven* is a vortex I sink through and am gone.

*

Surgery is a back-formation of *surgien*, a 13th-century Anglo-French word denoting something *worked, or done by hand.* As I lie insentient, the goings-on in my urogenital tract are a contemporary instance of such handiwork. For all the high-tech gear and tackle, one person again reaches out to another in the age-old ritual of healing. Surgery was performed in the Dakhla Oasis, following protocols laid out in medical textbooks dating from 2900 BCE. The Parisian Barber Surgeon Guild was the 16th-century French equivalent of today's American Medical Association. Physicians of the time considered surgery beneath their station, so barbers, better equipped with sharp instruments than most others, stepped into the breach. On battlefield and in monasteries, palaces, and hospitals, barber surgeons removed bullets, amputated limbs, and performed many other services done by surgeons today.

Ambroise Paré was to the guild what the surgeon general is to contemporary American medicine. Known as the "father of modern surgery," he first brought to handiwork keen powers of observation and the rigor of the scientific method. Writing not in the traditional Latin but in the French vernacular, his pioneering work influenced a wide audience of fellow barber surgeons. Paré explained to them that surgery had five objectives: *To remove what is superfluous, to restore what has been dislocated, to separate what has grown together, to reunite what has been divided, and to redress the defects of nature.*

Lying comatose on my *table d'opération*, I'm touched by many hands above and beyond those of my oncologist. May what is superfluous be left behind when I stand back up.

*

Stupendous pain. That's everything. Followed, seconds later, by awareness of a body that's the vehicle for this pain. Followed by awareness of that body's midsection as the pain's epicenter, from which it emerges like rays from a sun. Only after this comes the awareness *I'm awake.*

I groan. A nurse is sitting 30 feet away at a desk in the recovery room. Hearing me, she looks over and says, "You're awake." I don't know how to respond to this statement. I don't know how to do anything. I'm lying on a bed of exquisitely sharp nails. Any movement of body or mind increases my anguish. "How's your pain?" she asks. "On a scale of one to ten?"

I ponder this question. Pondering requires enormous effort. Could I experience any greater pain? I can't imagine it. It seems, dimly, this *is* a possibility. "Nine," I tell her from across the room. My voice is an uncanny mixture of whisper and scream.

"Well, don't tense up," she snaps back, still seated at the desk. She sounds annoyed. "Tensing up will only make it worse."

*

Julie is holding my hand. This doesn't hurt. I focus on this. I'm trying to see into her eyes, which are oddly far off in some dark middle distance. The nurse walks over, pushes another bolus of morphine into my drip line, walks back into the dark. Within a minute, the pain starts to recede. Followed, quickly, by everything else.

Already in free fall through the rabbit hole of today, my next exit doesn't surprise me. Another everyday occurrence in Wonderland.

*

Later that afternoon, Julie tells me this: "Shortly after the nurse left, you stopped breathing. Your eyes rolled back. Your head fell onto your chest. I thought you'd died. I started yelling and a bunch of people ran over and pushed me out of the room. I burst into tears and told Michael, 'Something really bad just happened.' He looked horrified, jumped up, and we hugged each other. Everybody else in the room, waiting their news, looked pretty bad too."

*

I may or may not officially have died. The medical record of the next minutes is scant. "Patient was quickly revived. It was decided to admit the patient for observation overnight." I share a hospital room with another patient, neither of us in any condition to chat—nor even to sleep. I lie awake all night listening to the nighttime beeps and pages, watching lights flicker on screens beside my bed, getting poked and prodded every hour by another nurse or orderly. I've been given a synthetic opiate and am in no pain. I am, in fact, euphoric.

"Now I get why people abuse opiates," I tell Julie when she arrives back at the hospital with breakfast. "Whatever else is happening, drop some dope into the equation *and all shall be well, all shall be well, all manner of things shall be well.*"

*

Up to a point, anyway. At discharge I'm given a bottle of opioid painkillers and told to take one every four to six hours, whether I'm in pain or not. "Don't wait until you feel pain," the nurse warns. "That will be too late."

Ever the good patient, I follow these directions. Until, a day later, I realize that while my pain levels are low, so is the rest of my experience of post-operative life. The October sky blazes blue behind the golden cotton-woods. The quails' sharp cries pierce the dry, sage-scented air. The fall constellations wheel fiercely through the night sky. And all this is happening *over there.* I'm disconnected from it in my opiate haze, dissociated, *out of place.* Also constipated, dry-mouthed, working harder to breathe than I remember having to.

I decide to stop the painkillers. Waking from a nap, six hours since my last pill, I lie in bed taking in a new experience. A sensation is growing in my midsection, radiating out from there through the rest of my structure. I decide not to judge this sensation, not even to name it. Just to observe it, with curiosity, and see what happens. It grows increasingly intense, vivid, present. A tingling that becomes a buzzing, as might emanate from a beehive.

*

Our peripheral nervous system contains the starting points for the experience we call pain. Specifically, it contains

47

three types of *nociceptors*—nerve cells that fire in response to mechanical, thermal, or chemical changes in surrounding tissue. This firing, known as *nociception*, travels to the spinal cord and from there to the brain, where multiple regions process the message. If the brain concludes the body is at risk, it will respond by producing the experience we call pain. If the brain decides the body is not in danger, the exact same signal will not produce any pain at all. Pain, then, is a protective mechanism. The exact same stimulus may or may not produce pain. It all comes down to the brain's perception of risk.

At discharge, the nurse set three expectations that I didn't notice until now, lying in bed painkiller-free a day later. What were they? *You will experience pain. Pain is dangerous. You must kill it before it kills you.* All those brain regions that process nociception were in the room, paying close attention, doing what they do best—figuring out how to protect me. Noticing as well that I was being advised by a medical authority, an expert, whom all believe knows better than does Daniel about such things.

Expectation has a way of becoming self-fulfilling: that which we await has a higher chance of occurring, simply because we expect it. Now, lying in bed, replacing expectation with curiosity, my brain has a bit more room to operate. A lot more room: there are more possible connections between my brain's 100 billion neurons than there are atoms in the known universe. In such a vast space, anything can happen. Here's what happens:

As the buzzing intensifies, I realize something astonishing: *it's not a problem unless I make it one.* It's simply sensation, neuronal firing in a healthy body, nociception. Labeling it *pain* instantly turns it into a problem, something I must brace and protect myself against, kill. I settle into this new experience, relaxed, still somewhat astonished, comfortable, secure. Within minutes I'm again asleep.

*

Having slept a lot today, I'm not sleepy when Julie's ready to turn in. I look into her face and see there exhaustion, concern, love, relief. Once she's in bed, I pull a long scarf through the handle atop my catheter bag and tie it over my opposite shoulder, bandolier style. I think of Pancho Villa. I think of Mr. Quinn. The surgeon wants me catheterized for five days to keep pressure from building inside my bladder, which could lead to its rupture. It's an ungainly lifestyle, this externalized internal plumbing. The catheter is kept from slipping out of my bladder by a bulb at its tip that's inflated with water. My surgery site is directly adjacent to this bulb and when I move in particular ways the two contact each other. Julie hears one result of *this* nociception from across the whole house.

I step outside. There's a new (that is, no) moon. From north to south horizons, the Milky Way drapes the sky. In the company of his billion bright fellow travelers, Pegasus stamps directly overhead. I've looked into this sky my whole life—in awe, admiration, astonishment. Tonight I feel something new: blessing. The sky itself, my standing alive beneath it, the whole big picture of this point in spacetime registers as an overwhelming *gift*. Tears come to my eyes, my body's response to the giving. I realize this gift has been every moment of my living-cum-dying. Realize that, somehow, I've managed not to receive, not to accept this gift. Managed to live half a century and miss the whole point.

CARE

From Old English caru, cearu: *"sorrow, anxiety, grief."*

Twelve days have passed since surgery. Julie and I are back at the medical center to get the pathology report. Post-op has brought its own challenges. Once the catheter was removed I developed a urinary tract infection. The itching and burning started on a Friday and the surgeon's office said I'd have to wait to see him on Monday to get a prescription for a round of antibiotics—which made for a long weekend. We are living day and night with the awareness that the report could say anything. That I'm cancer-free, released back into life like a cutthroat back into its native stream. That cancer has metastasized and has rooted elsewhere in my body. Or something in between.

Walking into the hospital complex, I stop, take Julie's hand, and look into her eyes.

"Whatever they tell us, we're going to be all right," I say.

Her eyes brim with tears. "Maybe *you'll* be all right," she replies.

*

The answer we get is *something in between.* The tissue sent to the lab did not contain muscularis propria, the layer of connective tissue between the tumor and the outside of the bladder. Without it, the pathologist couldn't tell whether or not the cancer had grown through the bladder wall. In short, the surgeon didn't send pathology what it needed to make a definitive determination of stage. He tells us he needs to do a second surgery.

*

Julie and I walk back outside and stand, dazed, in the late sunlight. Something in addition to muscularis propria has gone missing. Perhaps some expression of emotion. Regret? The surgeon's recognition that he didn't deliver what he'd said he would: *clean margins.* Without yet articulating it, we're feeling both these absences. The requisite tissue. The requisite human gesture. When Julie speaks I realize she is, per usual, a couple steps ahead of me.

"We're done with these people," she says quietly. I'm grateful for the steel in her voice. It steadies me in a world again coming off its footings. Hearing her words, I realize I quite agree.

Once home, Julie lights up her network. A researcher in mind-body medicine, she has colleagues worldwide who are subject-matter experts across a wide range of disease and wellness. Two days later she speaks with one of them, a physician himself diagnosed with bladder cancer 12 years earlier. He gives her the name of an oncologist in Phoenix. "It's simple," he says. "Have Daniel go see Don and do whatever he says."

*

Ambroise Paré and his fellow *chirurgiens-barbiers* brought to battlefield medicine the weaponry of battle. Sharpened steel punctured and sliced French soldiers in manly efforts to kill them—then again punctured and sliced in attempts to keep them alive. In the 20th century, sharpened steel played an outsize role in many of One Nation Under God's wars, not least its *War on Cancer*. Many human parts got lopped off. When the enemy regrouped and returned, standard operating procedure was more lopping. If radical mastectomy failed, lymph nodes followed. A colleague once said, "If all you have is a hammer, a whole lot of things look like nails." He was describing *The Law of the Instrument*, a cognitive bias that limits one's sense of possibilities to tools already at hand. In much of One Nation's 20th-century war on cancer, that instrument was the scalpel.

As the century progressed, other battlefield technologies were enlisted in the war. Though poison gases were outlawed by the Geneva Protocol in 1925, One Nation continued to manufacture and stockpile them. This came to light in December 1943 when German forces bombed a flotilla of US warships docked in the Italian port of Bari. Unbeknownst to its crew, one ship held 2,000 bombs filled with liquid mustard gas. In the Great War, mustard was known as *King of Battle Gases* due to its devastating effects on human tissue. The spilled Bari mustard formed a slick on the water that surviving sailors swam through to shore. Over the next days, they were plunged into mysterious agony: their skins blistered, they struggled to breathe, their noses bled, they vomited and lost vision. One Nation's military leaders denied any knowledge of what might be afflicting its sailors, leaving local medical personnel the job of working backward from these symptoms in an effort to determine their cause.

While the immediate effects of exposure to mustard were known, the incident spurred examination of long-term consequences. Researchers found Bari survivors' bone marrow and lymph cells significantly depleted. Pharmacologists at Yale University initiated animal studies that found similar effects on lymph cancer cells: nitrogen mustard triggered remission of lymphoid tumors in mice. Nitrogen mustard was next administered to patients with non-Hodgkin's lymphoma, leading to reduced tumor size in this cancer. In the decade following the second war, *chemotherapy*, as it came to be called, was touted by its advocates as the long-sought turning point in the war on cancer. Instead of more brute lopping, human tissue would be saved by injecting it with poison chemicals. While this sounds wrongheaded at first blush, it took time and clinical data to confirm this impression. Remissions for the most part were temporary. Chemotherapy failed to produce significant reductions in mortality for most cancer patients.

Atomic power was another 20th-century battlefield technology recruited in the war on cancer. *Radiotherapy* had been initiated for skin and other cancers shortly after the discovery of X-rays at the end of the 19th century. Radiation posed somewhat different problems than did chemotherapy. For one, while radiation is spectacularly effective at killing cancer cells, it is spectacularly effective at killing all other cells as well. *Collateral damage* is a term the military uses to describe human beings unintentionally killed or maimed in the course of the intentional killing and maiming of their family members and neighbors. There was a lot of collateral damage in the early decades of radiotherapy. And there were other problems as well. While a proton beam can successfully eradicate a local tumor, it does nothing to address micrometastasis—collections of cells shed from that tumor that travel, root, and grow elsewhere in the body. Then there's the awkward fact that radiation is *mutagenic*. That is, radiation can trigger in surviving cells the very genetic changes that drive cancer in the first place.

"War is hell," William Tecumseh Sherman said in the course of his 1864 March to the Sea. One hundred years later, the mounting body counts in the War on Cancer quite often proved him right.

*

Seventeen thousand years ago, a bison in what today is Wyoming succumbed to a bacterial infection. That same bacterium killed a mother and child buried together 9,000 years ago in a Mediterranean city itself now buried beneath the sea. The disease this pathogen causes has traveled under many names: *phthisis* in classical Greece, *tabes* in Caesar's Rome, *schachepheth* in early Hebrew. In 18th-century Europe it was called *white plague* on account of the bloodless look of its victims: their pallor led to the belief the disease was spread by vampires. It killed one in four Europeans during the Enlightenment. At the end of the 19th century, the German microbiologist Robert Koch isolated this infectious agent and dubbed it *Mycobacterium tuberculosis*, after its cylindrical shape. While Koch's discovery moved forward efforts to treat the disease, tuberculosis went on to kill more people during World War I than did all the bullets, bombs, and poison gas. Even today it kills more people worldwide than any other infectious disease.

In 1900, the newly founded Pasteur Institute in northern France began searching for a tuberculosis vaccine. Researchers Albert Calmette and Camille Guérin attenuated the bovine form of the bacterium to remove its more virulent genes and in 1913 began testing a vaccine in cattle. Encouraged by the results, they moved on to human trials, beginning in 1921 with oral administration to a newborn child whose mother had died of tuberculosis shortly after giving birth. The vaccine, named *Bacille Calmette-Guérin* (BCG) after its founders, proved both safe and effective, giving the world its first protection against this ancient, deadly foe.

In the years following World War I, Johns Hopkins biologist Raymond Pearl noted that tuberculosis patients, at autopsy, had significantly lower rates of cancer than other patients. His 1929 paper posited "a definite antagonism between the two diseases... only rarely does an active and considerable tuberculosis coexist with a malignant neoplasm in the same individual." In the following decades, Pearl's work led to animal studies that found BCG inoculation reduced the occurrence of a variety of cancers.

In the 1960s, the UCLA oncologist Donald Morton began injecting BCG directly into skin cancers and found this led to the destruction of 90% of these lesions. Significantly, 17% of injected patients also experienced regression in *uninjected* lesions. And one third of treated patients remained cancer-free at six-year follow-up. BCG seemed to offer the upside of other cancer therapies—targeted destruction of tumors *and* systemic effects—with few or none of such downsides as collateral damage of healthy tissue.

Thus a new era in cancer treatment, *immunotherapy*, was born. Instead of lopping, poisoning, and nuking the enemy, immunotherapy worked *with* one of the most complex, subtle, and powerful forces in the universe: the human immune system. Worked hand in hand with *Way-Things*. In the mid-1970s, immunotherapy took off in One Nation. The Vietnam War had ended. Earth Day became an annual celebration. Peace seemed to be breaking out all over.

*

In developing their vaccine, Calmette and Guérin followed in the footsteps of their fellow countryman Louis Pasteur. Introducing the body to a weakened form of the mycobacterium gave the body the upper hand in responding to and defeating it, averting development of the disease. But initial victory is not the point of vaccination. Vaccination "trains" the immune system to recognize and quickly respond to that particular pathogen going forward. In part, this training involves the formation of *memory cells*, lymphocytes that linger in the body long afterward and mount a fast-tracked, vigorous response to any future exposure to the mycobacterium. Vaccines are, in other words, *prophylactic* interventions, designed to prevent disease, not cure it. A vaccine won't help a patient already suffering from an infectious disease.

UCLA's Morton and others began investigating "off-label" uses of BCG. Instead of using it prophylactically to prevent bacterial infection, they began testing it *therapeutically* in already sick patients—in this case people diagnosed with cancer. Used therapeutically, BCG has an extended mechanism of action. Introduced into the body at a particular site, it provokes an immune response there when the body identifies the weakened mycobacterium as "not me." The body rallies immune cells to the site, including T cells, macrophages, and natural killer cells to clear the pathogen. Thus far, the response mirrors that of BCG used as a vaccine. But used therapeutically, BCG's effects continue. It provokes ongoing immune responses that include cytokine storms that bear such proteins as tumor necrosis factor and interferon gamma to the site. These agents in turn attack and (hopefully) kill cancer cells the body also recognizes as "not me." As Morton noted, some BCG also enters the bloodstream, where it produces anti-cancer effects elsewhere in the body.

*

In the summer of 1973, Donald Lamm and his wife were sunning on the beach with friends at Hanauma Bay, Hawaii. A first-year medical resident at the University of California San Diego, Lamm had spent the academic year inducing carcinomas in rat bladders. As the resulting tumors were microscopically quite similar to human bladder cancers, they gave UCSD researchers a mechanism for preclinical investigation of cancer therapeutics. Lamm had been invited to Honolulu to present two bladder cancer case reports at an American Urological Association conference. Between the snorkeling and sunscreen, a colleague about to retire from the field said, "Don, you've been going into the lab and making bladder cancers. Why not put BCG in those rat bladders to see if it will work?"

Upon returning to UCSD, Lamm did as he'd been told. He placed BCG directly into the bladders of his cancerous rats. Among body structures, a bladder is uniquely suited for this form of therapy. Via the urethra, it is open to the outer world. And, of course, its entire *raison d'être* is to retain fluid. Lamm hoped to find, as Morton had with melanoma, that the vaccine led to bladder tumor regression.

It didn't.

"But I'm stubborn," Lamm told me. Patiently working by trial and error, he eventually found a dose of the vaccine that did produce tumor regression. He took the new protocol through the necessary human trials, winning FDA approval of BCG as a new cancer therapy in 1990.

Don told me the Hanauma Bay story by way of answering a question. I'd asked how it was that, in 1979, he'd been awarded the first-ever National Institutes of Health grant to evaluate BCG as an immunotherapy for human bladder cancer.

"It wasn't my idea," he promptly replied. "Dave McCullough suggested it to me there on the beach." As often happens, Don's answer told me rather more than the sum of its parts. Put differently (and in words Donald Lamm would never use), he was saying, *I got the grant by being more into my work than into myself.*

Excellent thing, this. Before Don's work led to BCG becoming the gold standard for bladder cancer treatment, the recurrence rate for the disease was close to 100%. If you had one tumor, you *would* have more. Lopping, in this case, amounted to weeding a garden. As a result, cystectomy—surgical removal of the entire bladder—was often recommended to bladder cancer patients. For men the procedure also involved removing the prostate and seminal vesicles. Women lost their uterus, ovaries, and part of their vagina.

Talk about collateral damage! In the last three decades, BCG has rewritten the global bladder cancer story. Despite increasing *incidence* in the world population, bladder cancer is one of only five cancers whose mortality has *decreased* during that period. Reduced as well is the number of cancer patients who've lost their bladders due to progression of the disease.

Grandma Irene's immune system killed her. Thanks to Donald Lamm, her grandson's immune system just could save his life.

*

Before our first meeting with Don, we meet his medical assistant, Jamaka. Earlier in her career, Jamaka was an army medic, which might explain the martial spirit she brings to her work.

"Welcome to BCG Oncology," she tells Julie and me after marching us into a consultation room. "Here's the deal. We hate cancer here. We love to kill it. If we don't have what we need to kill yours, we'll invent it. Any questions?"

Julie and I look at each other and blink. "No, ma'am, no questions," I say, a slow grin spreading across my face.

"Good," Jamaka says. "Sit tight. The doctor will be in shortly."

When she's gone, I turn to Julie. Her face is a picture of astonished relief. "I think we've found the right place," I say.

*

"Breathe," Don says to me, quietly, patiently, good-naturedly. His tone is the full opposite of the recovery room nurse after my first surgery.

I'm lying on his exam table, my heels in the stirrups. Standing between my legs, Don has brought the light and camera crew up to the first urethral sphincter, a band of voluntary muscle that closes down on the urethra and controls the exit of urine from the bladder. When we're frightened or in pain, this muscle (along with many others) contracts. In August, my first urologist forced his cystoscope through this clamped space, producing the scream Julie so clearly heard in the waiting room.

Don waits. Hearing the warmth in his voice, feeling his comfort with waiting, I follow his advice. After a couple deep breaths, my muscles relax and the light and camera crew continue up, through my prostate, past my second urethral sphincter, and into my bladder. A flat-panel monitor beside the bed shows the inside of the organ, glowing a soft gold in the artificial light. We look at the surgery site—a raw, ragged battleground—then tour the rest of this inner world. Satisfied, Don removes the scope and asks when I want to have him do the surgery.

"How soon can I get in?" I ask.

"I have a slot next Tuesday morning," he says.

"I'll be there."

*

Tuesday morning. Julie and I have traveled home, packed what we figure we'll need, and returned to Phoenix. Our friends Russ and Sue invited us to stay in their guest suite, just down the street from the medical center. We got in last night, unpacked, and rose before dawn to get to the hospital. We're met there by a volunteer named Cynthia, who walks us through the registration process and offers to be our liaison with staff, all of whom she knows by name. Cynthia looks to be in her seventies. She tells us her husband received wonderful care at this center before his cancer death two years ago. She now gets up before dawn three days a week to help other families navigate the complex. "It's my way of giving back," she explains.

Cynthia goes to get an ETA on pre-op, and I take Julie's hand. It's warm and moist, like her eyes.

"How you doing, sugar?"

A tear rolls down her left cheek.

"This is so hard," she says softly. "This is the hardest thing I've done."

"You have the hard part," I tell her.

She nods, then looks around the clean, well-lit space and our early morning fellow travelers. "And this is *so much better* than that last place." She shudders, remembering last month's horrors.

Was it only a month ago? It was. Time seems to have come disconnected from its events. Or, amber-like, altogether ceased to flow: a media in which specific moments hang suspended. An image on an exam room screen. One sentence in a conversation. A line in a pathology report. The touch of a hand. A tear.

Cynthia returns with a nurse. I hug Julie and follow the nurse back to a small room, where I take off my clothes, put on a paper gown, and lie down on a gurney. The nurse returns, takes my vitals, and starts an IV. Larry, my anesthesiologist, comes in with his assistant, John. Larry is built like young Arnold Schwarzenegger, has a wide-open face, and exudes an air of *this is going to go just fine*. Within two minutes, I'm chatting with him as easily as once I chatted with Gregory Wertz.

The operating room nurse arrives with a surgical tech. Somebody is pulling compression socks onto my feet, somebody pushing something into my IV. A patient advocate stops by, then Cynthia arrives with Julie in tow. Julie's eyes widen and she pushes herself into a corner to be out of the way of the action. I reach out my hand and she comes and takes it, then starts telling Larry about our misadventures with anesthesia at my last surgery. He listens carefully, then tells us the names of the drugs he'll use and what each will do. He says he and John will keep a close eye on things.

Don walks in and talk drops off. The captain has stepped aboard. He smiles at me from the foot of the bed and asks if I have any questions. I think for a moment. "Doc, will I be able to play the piano when you're done?" Now he thinks for a moment. "Just as well as you do right now," he says.

Suddenly everything starts happening at once. Julie kisses my head and is gone. The room clears out and two techs roll me down a long hallway and through double doors into the operating room. It's cold in here. The walls are green, the floor white tile. More gowned figures fiddle with machines and take things out of drawers. I'm transferred to the operating table below the formidable, still-dark surgical lighthead. Electrodes appear on my chest and arms, and I see my pulse on the EKG screen. Someone slips a small mask over my nose and mouth, and I feel the oxygen flow in.

Larry's smiling face appears over me. He puts his hand on my arm and asks if I'm ready to party. I love this man. "So long as it's with you and Don," I tell him. He grins and says he'll start adding gas to the oxygen flowing into my mask. That I'll smell it and feel a bit dizzy. "Count backward from ten," he says, his hand still on my arm.

Ten. Nine. There's the gas. Eight. Seven. Yeah, kinda dizzy. I start telling Larry about it…

*

"Surgery will take two or three hours," Cynthia tells Julie. They're sitting together in a waiting area for family members and friends. "The surgeon will come out and talk to you once he's done."

"The last time we did this, they almost killed Daniel," Julie says. She tells the story of the first surgery. Cynthia looks shocked. She says that while anything can happen, Julie can expect much better results this time around. She says she'll be available till Don reappears. "Can I get you some coffee?" she asks.

She can.

*

Anyone who's experienced it will confirm cancer is a family disease. At every turn, it touches all parties—just differently. The light and camera crew, this time with blowtorch in hand, is currently navigating up my downstream. Eight people crowd around the proceedings, from which I'm mercifully absent. Julie sits alone with her thoughts, her fears, her hopes. Also not alone. Cynthia stops by. Julie calls her sister in Texas. My sister in Oregon. She gets texts from family and friends. At last count, 20 people said they were praying, in five different religions, for a good outcome.

Two hours in, Julie goes across the street to bring back lunch. When she returns, Cynthia tells her Don had come out looking for her. That he'd be back soon. When he returns, he takes Julie into a small, softly lit room with a loveseat on one wall, a table, and two chairs. He tells her the surgery went well. That he believes he got the margins the first surgeon didn't. That if pathology confirms the cancer hadn't invaded the muscularis, he'll recommend starting BCG treatment in about six weeks.

The first surgeon had spoken briefly with Julie in a busy hallway under fluorescent lighting. He spoke quickly, appeared rushed, seemed annoyed when Julie asked questions.

"Don seemed to have all the time in the world," Julie tells me later. "He's very kind. Present. Completely down-to-earth. Really *there* for me. I know he had a surgery waiting, but you'd never guess it from talking to him. He told me what to expect when we got back to Russ and

Sue's house, answered my questions about the logistics of travel and starting BCG. I understood this wasn't just his job. He really wants to help us."

"Any other questions?" Don asks.

"No," Julie says, standing up and hugging him. "Thank you."

"You're very welcome. The nurse will take you back into the recovery room when Daniel is awake."

*

"The surgery is all finished," a voice says. "It went well. How's your pain?"

"Pain?" I ask.

"That's what we like to hear," the voice says.

Gradually the room comes into focus. The woman who owns the voice. Coming out of general anesthesia is unlike waking from sleep. Sleep comprises stages, transitions, dreams—in other words, duration. Anesthesia altogether stops time. We wake from anesthesia as Rip Van Winkle awoke from his nap, astonished to find his musket rusted, his beard a foot long, his faithful dog gone. We take the word of those around us—this happened—and go forward from there.

Julie comes in, looks at me closely, takes my hand and kisses my head. The nurse begins showing her a catheter kit, explaining how to use it to flush the line should it become blocked by debris from the surgery. I'll have the catheter in place for three days. Anything could happen.

"The other docs don't send patients home with these," she says. "They just tell them to go to an emergency room."

"I guess Dr. Lamm considers what that trip might involve," Julie says.

*

Back at the house, I feel relief, gratitude, only a bit of pain. I prop myself at the table with Julie, Russ, and Sue and eat some dinner. Afterward I step out into the warm darkness and do tai chi on the pool deck. A waxing gibbous moon glows rose-gold in the east.

Julie comes outside and looks me over. "This is amazing!" she says.

"Yup," I tell her. "Thank you, Larry. Thank you, Don."

"Amen."

"Thank *you*, sugar."

Julie takes my hand, gingerly avoiding the catheter line. We stand, a little wobbly, two small figures on the surface of a small planet, gazing up into everything else.

Spiritual Exercise

Sickness before death is a very appropriate thing...
those who don't have it miss one of God's mercies.
                                        Flannery O'Connor

Ignatius Loyola, 16th-century founder of the Jesuit order, would not have been voted "most likely to be canonized" by his Basque Country classmates. The youngest of 13 children, he was baptized Íñigo, which translates as *little one*. His renaming himself as a young adult Ignatius, *fiery one*, suggests the future saint may have suffered from a condition Dad called "little man's disease." Biographers tell us Íñigo's adolescence was marked by braggadocio, open carry of weapons, street brawling, and stone-cold womanizing. Class privilege may have been all that saved him from criminal prosecution and prison. At 17 he joined the Spanish army, which made full use of his thuggish bent. He fought unscathed for the next decade, with a penchant for scathing others that won him the title *servant of the court*. Ignatius seemed destined for a career of martial glory quite in line with his childhood hero of "Song of the Cid."

Then came the May 1521 Battle of Pamplona. A French cannonball ricocheted off a stone wall and shattered Ignatius's right leg, ending his military career and nearly ending his life. Following a lengthy convalescence that left one leg shorter than the other, the former warrior limped off to a very different existence. In 1522, Ignatius went on retreat at the Benedictine abbey of Montserrat. He confessed his sins, gave away his princely clothing, and lay down sword and stiletto at the Virgin's altar. From Montserrat, he walked to the nearby town of Manresa, where he did manual labor at a hospital in exchange for room and board. During this time, he spent many hours alone in a mountain cave, fasting, meditating, and creating a new method of Catholic retreat, the *Exercitia Spiritualia* or Spiritual Exercises.

Four centuries later, Dad, a graduate of Loyola University, took me along on a fall retreat to Manresa Retreat House in the San Gabriel Mountains east of Los Angeles. I was 17. Like Íñigo, I was immortal and a bit thuggish. Like Íñigo, the seed of spiritual life lay somewhere in my breast. On that September weekend, with its daily schedule of *Exercitia Spiritualia,* that seed took root and began to grow. Latin prayers, incense, the gilt edges of the tall leather-bound volumes gleaming in the stained-glass library—these were the external elements of its soil structure. The internal elements were much older, reaching back to molecular forces at play in the superocean Panthalassa. It would take several decades—and collision with a lesser yet equally deadly missile, *urothelial carcinoma*—for that seed to come to fruition.

*

Flannery O'Connor wrote many stories of thuggishness and grace from her family's dairy farm in central Georgia.

68

A devout Catholic, O'Connor experienced the mercy of long sickness preceding her death from lupus at age 39. Her experience of living-cum-dying, like her daily life on a farm, provided essential context for her fiction. Alongside her Catholic faith, it also constituted the moral backbone of her fiction.

Her 1953 story *A Good Man is Hard to Find* concludes with a conversation between a grandmother and an escaped convict who calls himself The Misfit. The grandmother has lived in a state of superficial piety and concern for appearance that stands in the way of authentic relationship with even her own son and grandchildren. Following a car accident on a remote road in Georgia, The Misfit's henchmen take the grandmother's family one by one into the woods and kill them. Alone finally at the roadside with The Misfit, facing the imminence of her own death, the grandmother becomes increasingly desperate. She tries to sweet-talk the killer, offering him money and a cascade of pious platitudes. He ignores them all. Finally, *in extremis*, grace breaks through a lifetime of artifice. O'Connor writes the grandmother's "head cleared for an instant"— a wonderfully precise description of such moments.

"Why, you're one of my babies. You're one of my own children," the grandmother murmurs, reaching out and touching the man's shoulder. The Misfit springs back "as if a snake had bitten him" and shoots her three times in the chest. As his henchmen drag her body into the trees, he muses, "She would have been a good woman if it had been somebody there to shoot her every minute of her life."

*

In September 1939, as Europe descended into the cataclysm that became the Second World War, C.S. Lewis gave a sermon at Oxford University. Lewis, who had been wounded in the trenches during the First World War, told the congregation:

> *"The war creates no absolutely new situation: it simply aggravates the permanent human situation so that we can no longer ignore it. Human life has always been lived on the edge of a precipice... We are mistaken when we compare war with 'normal life.' Life has never been normal."*

"Life," one of my Zen teachers says, "is an emergency case." The word's Latin root is instructive: *emergere* translates as *arise* or *come to light*. Which is all that life ever does. There's nothing normal about it because life's each moment is unprecedented. Inimitable. Arising once, it will not rise again.

My first spiritual director was also the abbot of a Trappist monastery in Oregon. In his eighties, he contracted a rare, incurable blood disease. As his death drew near, a friend asked Bernard how he was doing with his dying.

Bernard, a wonderfully direct—that is, spiritual—man, replied, "I'm not sure. You see, I've never done this before."

There's the spirit any of us can bring to any moment of our living-cum-dying.

*

I'm sitting on the window seat in Mom's bedroom in the late afternoon sun. Her dog snores lightly at the foot of her bed. Mom just woke from a nap and we're talking about life since she was told she had inoperable liver cancer five years earlier. She was diagnosed at the age that, 25 years later, I myself would be diagnosed. She would die six months later, at the age I am as I write these words.

"Cancer is the best thing that ever happened to me," Mom says.

I'm too stunned to reply. *Is this some weird Catholic thing?* I ask myself. *Wanting to suffer like Jesus suffered? Is this her pain meds talking?*

Mom smiles and pats my hand. "Sounds ridiculous, doesn't it? And it's true."

*

A quarter century would pass before I realized what Mom was telling me. Realized she'd traveled a considerable distance from *At least we have our health.* Traveled much further than I had: I considered her cancer an unmitigated disaster. A still-young woman who neither smoked nor drank, was otherwise the picture of health, being told *We might slow its progress, but we can't stop it.* Mom was the college homecoming queen who married the college quarterback. The mother who raised seven kids. The artist who, once those kids were in bed, stayed up to paint and draw and cut glass tiles to create mosaics. Her kids grown, she embarked with Dad on a new life of blue-water sailing: Hawaii, Alaska, Acapulco. They'd be gone on their sailboat for months at a time. In that era before GPS and cell phones, Mom charted their course with compass and sextant, shooting sun sights by day and the night stars. And now, toward the end of so many excellent adventures, she'd discovered the very most excellent was terminal cancer.

How so? Until I myself was diagnosed I couldn't have answered. Today I can. Mom discovered, as did I, that in letting go of health, letting go of the body and its trenchant life, we enter freedom. Freedom from what?

From what we call illness and health. Call past and future. Call living and call dying. All these will be taken from us soon enough. Why not release them now and live out our days in the absolute freedom from which we arise and to which we return?

Yet I doubt that, without our diagnoses, Mom and I would have done this. Letting go is not an intellectual exercise. It involves our whole body, whole mind, whole strength. Even the saints among us seem to need the cannonball, the lupus diagnosis, the carcinoma. Need, as The Misfit noted, someone or something intent on killing us in order to enter into that goodness that is our true home.

We need one thing more: *willingness* to let go.

I work with terminal patients in my psychotherapy practice and see each make a fundamental choice. Informed they're dying, some patients demand remission, demand longevity, then become panicked, bitter, filled with despair. A cancer diagnosis increases suicide risk; my patients' denial of reality helps me understand why.

Other patients make an opposite choice. Releasing their grip on illness and health, living and dying, they free themselves, moment by moment, to live and to die. As they receive life, now too may they receive death. As one might an honored guest. As Francis of Assisi joyfully received "sister bodily death." These patients' last days are frequently among the happiest of their lives.

Illness before death is a very appropriate thing...

*

First light in northern New Mexico. The earliest ending of winter. A waning gibbous moon matte in the high, dry air. I'm standing in my driveway, hugging Julie goodbye before the day's drive south to Don's office in Phoenix. I see sadness, love in her eyes. Feel the fierceness in her clinging to me, the fierce beating of her heart. Breathe in the scents of sage and piñon, the morning sharpness of the world all around. From the purple robe locust a flicker's cry strings bright beads on the new light. A magpie's gun-metal-blue wing feathers glint in the sun. Each piece of rock in the gravel driveway stands in sharp relief, casting its unique shadow on its neighbor. The world emerging, moment to moment, facet by facet, never before seen, never to be seen again.

Don has asked me to come down each quarter so he can run the light and camera crew up the down staircase for a look-see. Bladder cancer is nothing if not persistent and Don wants to spot any recurrence sooner rather than later. So every 90 days I've been making the pilgrimage south and west, down the Colorado Plateau from my mountain home to the Sonoran Desert below. Cancer-free at my last two exams, I've stayed on for three weeks of BCG. I've come to view existence through this quarterly window. After each cysto I tell myself, *I have 90 days! What to do with them?*

I'm surprised how much I like this new, time-limited view of life. It focuses me in ways my pre-cancer perspective did not: on the bright particulars of a world emerging about me moment to moment. On those things I most want to do. On whom I most want to see. Three months is ample time to do what's important. It's also a familiar span: one season, daily movement from equinox to solstice and back again. One semester of school. In this rhythm I *engage* existence, indulge less dithering, less self-talk in the direction of *I'll get around to it sometime.* I also discover that not thinking beyond 90 days is a huge relief. Life is simpler, more straightforward. I acknowledge a cliff edge three months out. A topographical feature Don and I will walk up to, look over, and only then see what comes next.

*

I wake to the chitter of a cactus wren perched on a saguaro outside my window. The air is 20 degrees warmer than it was 24 hours and 6,000 feet ago. Due at Don's office at noon, I start the day by meditating.

Shikantaza is the Japanese term for my form of daily Zen practice. The word translates as "just sitting." If this sounds simple it's because it *is* simple. It's simplicity itself. If this sounds easy, you've never tried it. Shikantaza is the most challenging thing I do. Just sitting, we're not thinking. Not feeling, sensing, remembering, imagining—or anything else. In this condition body and mind fall away, leaving only a whole universe *universing*.

One can't dabble in Shikantaza. Dilettantes need not apply. We go all in or we don't go at all. We *buy the farm*. Shikantaza is the most challenging thing I do. The greatest pleasure.

*

As Catholicism has saints—extraordinary people like Ignatius and Francis—Zen Buddhism has bodhisattvas. Just as saints commit themselves to a code of conduct, an intentional way of life, bodhisattvas make vows expressive of their basic intentions. One such vow is to relinquish personal liberation (nirvana or entry to heaven) until all beings are liberated. As a young Zen student, I understood this as a kind of *putting oneself last*, an antidote to the self-promotion and line-cutting that characterizes too much Western life. As my practice deepened, I saw in this vow a more basic truth: there is no self separate from all other selves, all other beings past, present, and future. "Personal liberation" is an oxymoron—unless our experience of *the personal* is at once the widest and most intimate possible.

*

Two hours to my cysto. I breakfast, noticing the movements of my mind. Thoughts about the procedure and its discomforts. About what Don will find. About what I will do based on what he finds. Et cetera—from the Latin: *and the rest*. As in the *rest of the list* of possible thoughts. As if this list ever ends. As if one might think one's way to that terminus and be done. Be, finally, at rest. As in a musical *rest*. A stop. Stillness. Peace.

This never happens. I've discovered stepping onto this mind path is like stepping onto a hamster wheel. Discovered these rehearsals of possible futures add no value to my morning hours. Discovered that running security operations on life, I lose my life. Lose out on its arising in citric peaberry vapors from my coffee cup; in nut-flavored, chewy spoonsful of steel-cut oats; in the quick wailing of quail beneath the prickly pear outside. Life's sharpness clouds over, gets sullied with worries, craving, stress.

Here are some other sharp morning facts:

* I'm hoping for a clear bladder.
* This hope has been stable over time. I needn't check it moment to moment.
* In 300 minutes, I'll know if I'm clear or not.
* In either case, my 90-day clock will reset.
* One day I will die.

These facts, internal and external, comprise my context, my personal fact pattern. Particular to me this morning, they are not categorically different from anyone's fact pattern on any morning. They constitute the human fact pattern. *The war creates no absolutely new situation.* Nor does any other life threat. Such threats *simply aggravate the permanent human situation so that we can no longer ignore it.* If we no longer ignore the human situation, what will we do instead? Another way of asking the question: What's most important to me this morning?

Nota bene: The answer is *not* "a clear bladder."

*

What's most important to me this morning, or any morning, is a clear mind. Being clear with myself about the permanent (one could say *eternal,* one could say *timeless*) human situation. The principal work in this direction is clarity about 1] what lies within my reach; and 2] what lies beyond my reach. Reinhold Niebuhr's Serenity Prayer puts it thus: *God, grant me the serenity to accept the things I cannot change, courage to change the things I can, and wisdom to know the difference.*

Cognitive-behavioral therapy (CBT) provides ways and means of making Niebuhr's prayer to God a request of ourselves. Gives us a mechanism for granting ourselves serenity, courage, and wisdom—particularly when facing aggravated moments of reality. What does CBT bring to such moments?

Serenity to accept the things I cannot change. Almost all existence falls into this category. We might start with the weak nuclear force, with gravitational attraction. Move on to the weather, other people's opinions and choices, cellular senescence and death. Much more than 99.9% of reality lies beyond our control. Sitting in this room at my bread-and-breakfast, I may find myself uneasy. If so, it's certainly because I've not yet accepted certain things I can't change. My not already having the cystoscopy results. My vulnerability in the face of this un-knowing. The possibility of recurrence and the life-chang-ing cascade of events that follow from it. My death.

My nonacceptance will likely take the form of de-mands. *I have to be clear. I can't have a recurrence. I'm too young to die.* CBT provides cognitive tools with which to respond to such statements. A successful response will both cancel the demand and be highly believable. My re-sponse this morning is *I hope to be clear.* This response takes the demand out of the formulation and stays close to the fact pattern of reality. I might add, *And should I have a recurrence, I have as well a world-class team to address it.* Resetting my thinking in this way reduces or eliminates the physical stress and negative emotion created by my mental efforts to demand some particular version of real-ity. To bend the world to my will.

Courage to change the things I can. Everyone gets discouraged. For most of us, discouragement is a tempo-rary condition that soon passes. For others it becomes a chronic state. Some of us are actively discouraged from birth on by the people around us. We may go on to dis-courage ourselves our entire lives. We'll then view 100% of reality as unchangeable and live in states of helpless-ness and depression.

Here, too, CBT can help, this time with behavioral tools. It encourages patients feeling profound levels of helplessness to conduct experiments and gather data re-garding their actual capacity. This data generally heartens patients, leading them to continue exerting efforts to cre-ate lives worth living. For me this morning, such effort takes the form of writing notes about my experience in hopes that capturing these morning movements of my mind might help others facing such mornings.

Wisdom to know the difference. Now here's the rub! If serenity and courage are sides of a coin, we can't, unfortunately, simply flip it. Facing some great challenge, some aggravated moment in the human situation, which of these forks in the road to take forward might not be at all clear. We may no longer be good judges of our true capacity, or of its limits.

Social creatures at our best, we can sometimes clear the air by adding IQ points to the equation. Crowd-sourcing the choice. Reaching out to another human being. Time and again human relationship provides me a beacon to steer by. Enables me to navigate the storms of confusion and muddlement, to arrive at what is, finally, our only safe harbor: a clear mind.

All great world paths have serenity prayers. Taoism has one of my favorites. In his "Tao Te Ching," Lao Tzu writes "Less and less do you need to do, until finally, nothing is left undone." In this couplet, Lao Tzu combines Niebuhr's requests into a single formulation and life path. Being and doing, Lao Tzu says, aren't adversaries. Entirely engaging our lives, moment to moment, there is no longer a separate *one* doing something *other*. There is only the Tao, flowing through all beings, all moments of spacetime. Only a universe universing. In this condition—our true home—nothing is left undone. In ongoing acts of completing, we embody completion itself.

*

The morning sun feels good on my skin as I walk to the little park down the street. The cinderblock neighborhood was built up about the time I was born, when three bed-rooms, two baths, and 1,800 square feet were all most anyone needed. Yards are xeriscaped, with yucca and aloe vera and jojoba separated by stretches of brown and pink gravel. The occasional palm tree towers 40 feet overhead. The block exudes an air of tidiness, order, permanence.

A chain-link fence surrounds one home and a large dumpster is parked at the curb. Half of the home looks like the others on the block, half is a see-through assembly of charred studs and rafters. I think of my son, a fire paramedic, who runs *into*, not out of burning structures. Think of the color red: flames, trucks, emergency lights. Think of the shock of an entire neighborhood at this sudden transformation of a part of life whose presence everyone took for granted.

The park adjoins a schoolyard where a PE class is taking place. First-grade children, masked against pandemic, are running laps around the grass. A woman stands at the center of the circle, blowing a whistle, calling encouragement. The children's faces are serious behind their masks, eyes intent. There's no small talk, even between the two girls running hand in hand. All the energy in the place goes directly into running.

*

All great world religions are evolutionary pathways. Just as human physical structure emerged from the great fishes, the human mind developed from those of our earliest progenitors. This mental development precisely maps onto structural changes in the mammalian brain. As the neocortex took shape, reflexive consciousness arose: awareness of awareness itself. As it did, early hominids not only heard the saber-toothed cat roar, they also thought of *one hearing* that roar. That is, they became aware of a *me*. This was a huge step forward for our species, a sea change in the evolution of human experience. It corresponded with the rise of language and with all that followed from the spoken, and later the written word.

Shakyamuni Buddha's life embodies humans' next great step forward. Prior to Buddha, humans

79

exclusively identified with this *me*—with their physical structure and content of their minds. Early modern humans experienced body and mind as the start and finish of me: a separate entity, enwrapped in skin, set in opposition to the rest of reality. This opposition became the unexamined foundation of religious observance. *Me* appealed to the gods for longevity, successful harvests, salvation from hell. *Me* became as well the basis for literature, philosophy, medicine, physics, and every other field of human endeavor.

Then Buddha looked up from beneath the bodhi tree and saw the morning star. We could equally say the morning star looked down and recognized the young prince. In this most intimate encounter, Buddha saw through identification with a skin-wrapped body and mind. Looked deeply into that prior reality from which body and mind—and all things—arise. The Buddhist record reports that in this moment he exclaimed, "All beings are already enlightened! It's only delusive thoughts and feelings that obscure that prior reality." In the following centuries, sages East and West reported, in their own terms, this same breakthrough.

Thus did the next stage of human evolution emerge, one sometimes called the *transpersonal age*. Humans' experience of themselves began crossing over the skin barrier to embrace what had heretofore been but context. Embrace the rest of reality as oneself.

*

Modern cognitive science has identified the cortical structures involved in transpersonal crossing over. These include the medial prefrontal cortex, posterior cingulate cortex, and other interacting hubs and subsystems in the brain. Taken together, they're called the brain's "default mode network" and represent what the human brain does when it's not actively engaged in life. Running round a field, say. The default mode network represents the baseline state for the human brain at this stage in its evolution.

So what does the resting brain do? In a word: worry. About what? The content of the default mode can be summed up in one word: *me*. The brain's background noise is like a Greek chorus in constant, concerned comment about events unfolding before it. *What will become of me? What dangers await? How can I be safe?* If this sounds tiring, it is. The default mode consumes up to 80% of the energy consumed by a brain actively involved in *living* life. In running round a field. So while reflexive consciousness was a great step forward for humankind, it's now the greatest drag anchor against our next step forward.

Now the good news: we can weigh anchor. Western cognitive science is confirming, via functional magnetic resonance imaging, what the perennial wisdom has taught for millennia. Meditation—what Buddha did beneath the bodhi tree, what Christians call *prayer of the heart*—turns down activity in the default mode centers. Quiets the worried chatter. If we pray earnestly and well, like children running, we can turn completely off, leave behind this artifact of our evolutionary journey.

*

Harvest moon, equinoxial drifter, just risen, perfect orb, shimmering yellow-gold, pulsing through the evening vapors. Lighter elevations stand above darker seas, shadowed craters, sites of old impacts. A compelling, beautiful arrival, stepping forth moment to moment, commanding the dusky atmosphere…

I'm again lying, knees up, feet in the stirrups, on Don's examination room table. He's standing between my legs, holding in both hands the meter-long cystoscope, steering the light and camera crew like a lunar lander over the interior landscape of my bladder. The risen moon floats on a color screen set next to me in the darkened room. That's *me*, just risen, over there. Don, Jamaka, and I are on the outside looking in. I'm also on the inside, looking out—a double perspective that's always a bit dizzying. Jamaka's hand rests on my shoulder. Its warmth registers there the way I imagine a life preserver registers in the arms of a person overboard on the high seas.

I've walked to the edge of my 90-day cliff, and the three of us are now peering over. A network of blood vessels spiderweb the urothelial lining. Their presence is what makes early diagnosis so urgent: an aggressive tumor that grows through the lining would shed cells that could be carried anywhere blood flows, seeding new tumors. This seeding, called *metastasis*, can mark the beginning of the end for cancer patients.

The moon's surface ripples as Don palpitates my abdomen. Here's the prostatic urethra, complex interchange of male reproductive plumbing. Here's the site of my first surgery, a two-centimeter crater lying beneath the surrounding tissue. Here's the scar left by one of Don's biopsies. Here a ureter enters from its kidney above. This intimate landscape is as familiar to me now as my face in a mirror.

"Looking good so far," Don says. "We'll switch to UV." Ultraviolet light makes visible details that don't appear under visible light. Bladder cancer, the chief urogenital *Hey-Guys!*, is nothing if not furtive. Don, chief cop on the *Way-Things* beat, is nothing if not thorough.

"Just wouldn't be a party without black light," I tell him.

I watch the red blood vessels turn black, the urothelial tissue throb dense violet. Satisfied, Don snaps off the light. "Hallelujah!" he exclaims. "That is one healthy bladder!"

I feel the scope slither back down my innards. My body starts to relax. My clock resets.

In the days leading up to a cysto, almost beneath the level of awareness, tension quietly starts building. A kind of bracing. Against what? Recurrence, of course, and that cascade of events that would follow. Each time I pack the car, I put in the stuff we've learned we'll need if, instead of returning home, I return to the operating room. The music stand to which we hook the catheter bag beside my bed. The plastic mattress cover. The gauze and saline and bottles of pills. The loose-fitting clothing. Sleep gets restless for us both. Calendar events are penciled in, with plans B placed alongside. Family and friends call and text well-wishes, prayers, encouraging words.

Now the bracing lets go. Before leaving the exam room, I call Julie. I hear the trepidation in her voice.

"Hello?"

"Good news!"

"Thank God," she says. "I could cry."

*

Back outside the air-conditioned medical plaza, the spring sunlight lands soft and warm on my skin. The sky is fiercely blue, the yucca's emerald leaves blaze sword-edged against it, greener than when I walked by on my way in. From the mesquite's open branches, a grackle's whistle pierces the midday air. An old woman in bathrobe and bedroom slippers wrestles her walker down the sidewalk. Fluorescent-green tennis balls have been stuck to the walker's front feet. A tatty miniature poodle with a rhinestone-studded collar totters along on a leash beside her, the topknot on its head tied up in a new pink bow.

Hallelujah! Ninety days more! What a gift! What riches!

Gratitude washes through my body and mind. Tears sting my eyes. I'm the luckiest guy alive. I give thanks for my immune system, my bladder. For Don's *Hallelujah!* A guy who's not just doing some job. A guy with skin in the game. For Jamaka, her simple, full-on presence.

And so on. For the rats that died in Don's lab five decades ago. For a planet receiving my footsteps, sending its mass back up through my spine and into the empty sky. My body feels light, almost weightless: a first-grader running. Everywhere I look, everything I feel, hear, think registers as blessing. Default mode switched off, my brain directly receives the raw data of my living-cum-dying. The timeless good news.

Another of Mom's favorite saints, abbess and church doctor Catherine of Siena, lived, died, and taught from this place. "Each step of the way to heaven," she told her nuns, "is heaven."

Return

*We keep coming back and coming back
To the real: to the hotel instead of the hymns
That fall upon it out of the wind.*

Wallace Stevens

A ruby-throated hummingbird works the yellow cholla blossoms, waggling his outspread tail, chittering up and down Arizona morning's bright scales. He zooms over to inspect my red t-shirt, his wings' metallic zing bringing the whole yard to attention.

This is everything: this encounter. This tiny airman's downcurved bill probing the nectar. This blossom. This one. This glittered hovering, seraphic, inches from my heart. Another kind of probe?

Daniel! I stand naked before you on the air sustaining us both. See! My wings beat 100 times each pulse of your heart, in circle eights, symbol of eternity, lemniscate *in your language, figure traced by the sun in the course of a year, shape inscribed in 1,000-year Arab stone. Daniel! Name that means* God is my judge. *The lions are circling. Feel their hot breath. How are you, Daniel? With each, with everything?*

This is everything. This meeting of heart/mind. Our whole story. The rest is conjecture. Memory. Visions of some future. The rest has never, will never exist. So we keep coming back and coming back to *this*—to all that we'll ever have.

*

Return. From the Latin *re* and *tomare*: to turn back. As the earth this spring morning turns back from the night. Turns back from winter at this latitude, from all of history. As blossoms return to the cholla and jojoba and brittlebush ringing the yard. As I return once more with the season to this bed and breakfast to peer with Don and Jamaka over the edge of a cliff.

A leaf blower revs up in the yard next door. A plane gains altitude over the airport. The life of the city returns around me, as it has never once failed to do.

My cysto is scheduled for two this afternoon. Julie calls and asks how I'm feeling.

"Vulnerable," I tell her. "Fifteen percent at risk." Fifteen percent vulnerable feels about right, a good fit for my circumstances. I could, of course, lower it by doing some CBT. Mood is eminently pliable: with some basic understanding and a few cognitive tools, we can pretty much feel whatever emotion we want to feel under any circumstance. In fact, *at all times* we decide to feel whatever we're feeling—though many of us make this decision all willy-nilly, without much intention or awareness of what we're doing. Mood, under these circumstances, feels a lot like weather, a thing beyond our control. We fail to see our thoughts and actions driving it, as surely as the turbines in the engines overhead drive their jetliner into the morning sun.

Instead of adjusting my mood, I decide to work on a blog post. Do some tai chi down at the park. Check out the PE class at the grade school. Decide to enjoy, appreciate, this sensation of vulnerability. Appreciate the interdependent co-arising that is the structure of reality. I exist because all else exists. All else exists because I exist. We're in this together, this living-cum-dying. Patients, providers, hummingbirds, cholla blossoms. Because people get cancer, Don Lamm has his practice. One never exists without all others.

The moment we claim exemption from this reality, assert autonomy within it, is the moment we start to suffer. The moment we leave the fundamental security, the perfect support that is living-cum-dying—the blue palo verde standing in its morning pool of darkness and light—we enter alone the valley of the shadow of death.

Now, like stepping from still water at the edge of a stream out into the current, things move more quickly. I return to the B&B, pack my two bags, put them in the trunk of the car, take a quick look through the room and find my computer power cord still plugged into a wall, tell my host I'm leaving. He knows where I'm going and wishes me luck. Pointing the car toward Don's office, I roll through the now familiar neighborhood, past the once burned home down the street that is now standing whole in a fresh coat of paint.

On the way, I call my friend and colleague Steve. Steve discovered last year he has multiple myeloma, a very rare blood cancer. He thought he'd put his back out and was visiting chiropractors and massage therapists to address the pain. By the time he was diagnosed, 90% of his blood marrow was cancerous. Steve's receiving his monthly chemotherapy infusion up in Denver this morning and I want to hear how it's going.

"Great!" Steve tells me. "I got to cry with another patient at the clinic, a woman who's been just diagnosed. Such a blessing."

Interdependent co-arising. Perfect support. Blessing, indeed.

*

"NO WAY IN HELL HE'S GOING TO ANSWER THAT QUESTION!" roars a large woman draped in a floral muumuu, elbows propped on the receptionist's counter. All eyes in the waiting room lift from their magazines and phone screens. All breath is suspended. The brim of the woman's sunhat quivers with outrage.

"We're not the ones asking, ma'am," Don's receptionist says in a friendly tone. "Your husband has Medicare. It's a standard form they require all patients to complete."

"OUR SEX LIFE IS NOBODY'S BUSINESS BUT OUR OWN," the woman thunders, slamming her fist down on the counter. "ANYWAY, IF ANYBODY NEEDS TO KNOW, TIM GIVES THE BEST CUNNILINGUS IN THIS WHOLE VALLEY!"

Jamaka opens the waiting room door and nods at me. Our brown eyes meet. *Welcome to my world*, hers say, without further comment. It seems vulnerability doesn't always bring forth better angels. Don chuckles when he hears the story.

"I end up with the patients everybody else fires," he explains apologetically. Seems better angel is not a condition for entry to Don's shop.

I ask Don about his leaving a plum appointment at a prestigious academic medical center which recruited him on the basis of his groundbreaking work. I'd heard one reason he left to set up his one-man shop was that at the center it could be a challenge to treat patients on Medicaid.

"I came up—*unwealthy*," Don replies. "My dad's dad, who had a farm in Iowa, went to Bible college. He and one of my cousins were the only ones in my family who went to college. My own dad was a railroad man. So I guess I have a feel for folks like mine."

Unwealthy. It's a perfect Don word. He wouldn't look to distinguish his family nor the trajectory of his professional career with a word like *poor*. Wouldn't want to invest himself with some kind of *noblesse oblige*. It's just that he wants, in Jamaka's words, to kill cancer. Not rich people's cancer. Cancer.

*

"Actually, *I'm* the one who ends up with those patients everyone else fires," Jamaka tells me as she takes my vitals. "He comes in, does his thing, and leaves. It's me and the front desk who have to clean up the messes."

She dips a test strip into my urine sample, pulls it out, and nods approval. My temperature, too, passes muster. The pulse oximeter clipped to my finger reports blood-oxygen at 96%. My heart is beating 87 times per minute—high for me, except in an anteroom like this. Blood pressure, too, is running a bit high. My body knows where it is in space-time. *Welcome to the cliff edge.*

*

The exam room lights go down. The moon again rises on the screen to my right. Jamaka stands to my left, her hand on my shoulder. An instrumental version of Joni Mitchell's "Both Sides Now" plays softly over the office sound system. Don stands between the stirrups, expertly piloting the lunar lander over terrain now familiar to us all.

"Uh-oh," he murmurs softly. I look at the section of moon he's zoomed in on and see what looks like a cauliflower stalk emerging from the lunar surface.

"Looks like an early-stage papillary tumor," Don says. "Probably low grade. Let's see if there are any others."

My first thought: *This man often has the hardest job in the world.* Saying *uh-oh* to someone in his care, knowing better than anyone what might, what will follow.

I follow the rover for a bit, then look over at Jamaka. There are tears in her eyes.

I love each one of those tears. *Skin in the game. Interdependent co-arising.*

*

I generally have a couple cancer patients in my psychotherapy practice. Some feel depressed or angry. Most feel anxious and panicky. These patients rank high among my favorite people. Among the most real. When I was diagnosed, and had accepted the reality of my situation, I no longer saw any reason *to behave.* Any reason to do something because others might want me to. Every reason to do whatever the hell *I* most wanted. If not now, when? This *damn-the-torpedoes* spirit travels with cancer patients when we're at our best.

We're not always at our best. Most of us in remission get concerned about recurrence, particularly in the days leading up to a scan. We've even invented a word for it: *scanxiety.* This makes a fundamental kind of sense. If you've broken your leg once, you might well worry about circumstances that could break it again. For some cancer patients, this possibility becomes the central defining feature of life, crowding out other considerations. Now, instead of living life, a physically healthy person spends hours daily researching longevity on the internet, hanging out in chat rooms with other worried patients, scanning his or her body for signs of trouble.

Such patients' medical prospects are often quite good. They might face a 10% chance of recurrence in the next decade. Should their cancer return, there's a good probability it can again be treated. Chronically worried patients don't find security in such numbers. Somewhat unthinkingly, they identify with that ten percent. Five percent. Less-than-one percent. They just know they're *doomed*. Know that cancer is even now deploying its tentacles throughout their bodies. Know that, when finally discovered, it will have metastasized. That it will be *too late*. Over months and sometimes years, this position in the life stream comes to resemble that on death row. Except it's we ourselves who've delivered the death sentence.

Panicky cancer patients are uniformly smart. Uniformly kind and ethical. Anxiety tends to travel in such company. Sociopaths aren't often anxious or worried. It's the best people among us who are most vulnerable to irrational fear. Given enough bandwidth, we are able at the same time to live our lives and to scare the living daylights out of ourselves.

"I know the present moment is all I'll ever have," they tell me. "*Rationally* I know this. But that knowledge doesn't even touch this feeling of dread. They travel together."

Just so! When it comes to first questions, intellectual knowledge is a spectator at a soccer match. The action is on the field, not in the bleachers. Intellect never gets into the game.

It's at precisely this point that existentialists turn back. There's little chance of *thinking* one's way, in any satisfying manner, through the valley of the shadow. Think what we may, death stands before us, as adamant as the period at the end of this sentence. The opening line of Albert Camus's 1948 essay *The Myth of Sisyphus* reads: *Il n'y a qu'un problème philosophique vraiment sérieux: c'est le suicide.* "There is but one truly serious philosophical problem, and that is suicide."

I first read Camus in religion class at my Catholic high school—and immediately liked him. His honesty and *rigueur intellectuelle* distinguished him from the yes-men of my Catholic boyhood. The *because-the-pope-says-so* men. Camus comes at things directly, respectful of his reader. *You are capable of thinking for yourself,* his book told us seventeen-year-olds. *You will die. Please put these two facts together.*

Camus's admonition has lived long and well within the Catholic tradition. *Memento mori*—"Remember death!"—the early Church Fathers and Mothers advise us, both in their writing and in the example set by their lives. On Ash Wednesday the nuns would walk us down the street to church, where the priest smudged our foreheads with ash and murmured, *Remember, man, that you are dust, and that to dust you shall return.* Murmured it not only to me but also to Laurie Schulte, Lisa Hopkins, the identical twins Mary and Maureen McCarthy...

I thrilled to this message. Felt a strong, schoolboy tropism toward it. My pet turtles died. My fish went belly-up in their bowl. No one even tried to explain these events to me. Mortality, like sexuality, lay shrouded in uncomfortable silence. I realized by third grade I'd need to come to my own terms with sex and death. As had Camus. As had Tertullian. As had Mechthild. Running like a bass line beneath the birthday parties and basketball practices, this inquiry seemed a project eminently worthy of my attention. That moment one afternoon, standing in the garage of our home on Tristan Drive, that I realized I'd fallen hard and fast for Laurie Schulte, I realized something else: she and I both would die.

And so: How to live? What to do?

Sometimes my anxious cancer patients feel this same tropism, a desire to move beyond distracting themselves, beyond fearful avoidance and received wisdom about death, into something more direct. To find an alternative to addressing mortality as a thought problem. Those who earnestly take up this matter sooner or later relinquish thinking, relinquish the mind path as their road forward. They find instead some other way to take up this first question. Some path leading into the kingdom of direct experience. Doing so, they become, perhaps for the first time, candidates for the realization that they have always, at the bottom, been free of anxiety regarding dying and death.

What is the content of their realization? Always the content is this: the present moment is not only all that any of us *has*, it's all that any of us *needs*. The present moment contains everything. And because it does, we are absolutely secure right here, right now, regardless of our medical status or prognosis. Secure, in fact, no place else—in heaven, on earth or below the earth, in any other time past, present, or future. Perfectly supported—by tears, by touch, by gallows humor.

"It's so comforting to go to my multiple myeloma support group and see people doing so well," Steve told his wife, Barb. Barb considered this statement for a moment.

"Be that as it may, you could be getting a skewed view of things," she said.

"Whatcha mean?" Steve asked.

"Dead people don't attend support groups."

*

Don finds no more cauliflower in the patch. Which relieves us all. Curious, how experiencing something most patients dread, I feel relief. The Perennial Philosophy teaches it's less *what* befalls us than what we tell ourselves *about* what befalls us that gives events their emotional meaning. Nowhere is this more apparent than in the kingdom of cancer.

I called a colleague on her birthday. I'd heard her breast cancer had recently returned—and metastasized to her spine. She, too, had been visiting chiropractors and massage therapists, thinking her pain was muscle tension related to her stressful job.

"Happy birthday," I said. "How are you feeling?"

"Quite well," she promptly replied.

"That's wonderful!" I exclaimed. "How so?"

"It spread only to bone," she explained. "Not to any organs. Not to my brain."

*

Relief. *A single tumor. Likely not invasive. Almost certainly low grade.* This recurrence is not our first rodeo. As soon as the scope comes out, we go into action. Don goes to his office to check his surgery calendar. Jamaka calls the hospital to schedule the operating room. I call Julie, who calls family and friends. Jamaka comes back with a surgery date five days out and a script for the usual surgical supplies: antiseptic wash, antibiotic, pain meds, laxatives. I cancel my patients, cancel my classes, book another stay at the B&B, go for an afternoon hike among the saguaro, barrel cacti, and prickly pear at the Sonoran Mountain Preserve.

I feel confident: *We've so got this.* Feel grateful: *We caught it early.* Feel motivated: *Let's do this!* I want to place a finger on the scale pan *life.* Do what I can do.

I had a patient who had lived for months terrified about recurrence. As soon as she was rediagnosed, she relaxed. Now, instead of focusing on her fearful thinking, she focused on what she was able and willing to do. Doing so, she learned something essential. Something she might not have learned any other way. After her second surgery, she experienced little anxiety about further recurrences.

What she was able and willing to do. Might this be all the more focus that any of us needs to live and die well?

*

I shower the night before surgery, dutifully lathering up with antiseptic wash. Set the alarm for five a.m. so we'll be at the hospital by six. Tell Julie to remind me should I forget and start to drink something more. She nods, looking stressed. Resolute. We both know the drill by heart.

"We gonna do this thing?" I ask.

"Yeah," she sighs.

I pull her to me and hold her close. Feel her heart beating quickly. Or else my own.

I quickly fall asleep. Dream I'm on an upper floor of a large, multi-floor warehouse. A feeling of dread. Intuition there's something profoundly evil in this place. Something or someone coming for me. *I must get out of here!*

I run to the freight elevators and push the down button. The dial above the door shows the car is six floors down. And not yet moving. Now I realize whatever is after me is in the elevator next to the one I've called. I watch the dial above its door spin round like a sweep hand, floors one to twelve and back again. Whatever's in there is mocking me. *Hah! Think you can run? Watch this!*

Now that elevator's doors slam open and my heart stops. Suspended midair in the car is a ferocious, many-armed, scarlet figure sitting in the lotus position. Its eyes burn like black coals. Its skin glows like molten lava. It's entirely focused on *me.*

Life or death. I look desperately about for some means of defense. See a machinist's hammer lying on the floor and pick it up. The demon laughs aloud, a sound like sheet metal torn asunder. A machinist's hammer appears in its many hands, spinning round there fast as the tips of a baton in a twirler's fist. My heart sinks…

Now something shifts. Not in the demon; in me. I realize there's something I'm able and willing to do. I hurl my hammer directly at the demon's head. As it strikes, the demon disappears, leaving me staring into the empty car.

It's my own mind! I exclaim, waking up.

Relief—I dare say *enlightenment*—washes through me. *Mind may present these chimeras. I myself have been secure from the very start!* I lie in bed awhile, bathed in this security, perfect support reaching down to the blue depths of collective subconsciousness. On this night before cancer surgery. On any night on earth.

*

We wake before the alarm in early darkness. An owl woofs four times in the yard outside. Three woofs answer from further off. This call and response, Gregorian chant of the pre-dawn treetops, accompanies us as we get out of bed, dress, and make our way through the dusky yard to the car.

The streets are quite empty at this hour, a rare thing in present-day Phoenix. Julie drives without her GPS. This is our third pre-dawn trek to this same hospital. We're grateful to have it waiting amidst the saguaro at the city's edge. Julie drops me at the main entrance and goes to park in the garage. A volunteer I've not met, a woman in her sixties sporting a bright silk scarf, greets me with a broad smile. I feel myself relax, smile in return. Two couples sit together in the comfortable atrium. An elderly man sits alone along the back wall.

"Good morning!" the woman says. Her name tag reads Theresa. She looks happy to see me.

"Yes, it is!" I reply. "A great morning all around." The couples look up and smile. The old man continues watching the floor between his feet.

Theresa checks me into the system, asks if I have questions, says a nurse will be out shortly. Julie arrives and we sit together holding hands like the other couples. An easy silence fills the early hall. No muzak. Fresh-cut flowers. *A sense of peace.*

So this is how it goes. We're born, grow up, raise families of our own, grow old, collecting stories our grandchildren will pass down to their grandkids. Sooner or later we get summoned to this place, or one like it, to sit together in first light. Sometimes nodding a bit, almost returning to last night's sleep, *dozing in the depths of wakefulness* as Wallace Stevens once wrote of an old philosopher friend. You'd be forgiven for mistaking us for a docile bunch. For missing the bright fact that, here at the cliff edge of life and death, life burns fierce as it ever has in our soft and sagging breasts.

*

More fiercely than it ever has. How so?

We are born to the task of becoming ourselves. Becoming who we really are is our lifework. "God wants to be God in you," Eckhart tells us. God wants to be born, to age and to die in precisely each of us. Yet for some mysterious reason we spend much of life fighting God on this point. We primp and pose to prop up a *me* of our own design, an entity separate from and (we tell ourselves) equal to divine will. Living-cum-dying becomes a life-and-death struggle between egoity and divinity. Culture sides with egoity: posing captures the headlines.

What would winning this contest look like? It would look a lot like losing. Egoity surrendering to divinity. Surrendering, that is, to reality. Like a tree shedding its leaves, we can let go of primping and posing, let go of a lifetime's adornment. At the end of our days, in the deep winter of life, we stand like an ancient oak in mid-January, every leaf finally fallen, every bird flown its nest. Muscle tonus is such a leaf. Health is such a leaf. Sharp eyes and ears are leaves. Now, perhaps for the first time, our fundamental structure appears, clear and sharp against the snow.

One of my teachers, as an old woman, told me this about losing her visual acuity: "Perhaps now I'll just see what's essential."

*

Larry walks by in the hall outside the little stalls made by side curtains in the pre-op area. He does a double take, steps back, and sticks his head in. "You again?!" he exclaims. "What are you doing here?"

"We missed you and John so much," I tell him. "We'll pretty much do anything to get to party with you guys again."

"Are you scheduled for Daniel's surgery?" Julie asks a little breathlessly. She still has flashbacks from my post-op misadventure after my first surgery.

"Lemme look," Larry says. He returns a few minutes later and says, "Yup. I'm your guy."

"Thank God!" Julie says. "I've been praying we'd get you. I called your office but couldn't get through." Larry looks pleased, pleasantly embarrassed.

"I'll be with him the whole time," he tells her. "John too. Daniel's going to be just fine."

A bevy of nurses fusses about me: taking vitals, starting an IV, pulling compression stockings onto my feet, asking me what I'm here for this morning and writing my reply on a form. Amid the bustle, we share stories of recent vacations, hiking in Utah's Canyonlands, road trips through New Mexico's Indian Country. An older nurse with a slight British accent arrives and the mood in the room downshifts.

"What are you here for this morning?" the newcomer asks me in a Big Nurse tone. A tone that says she expects to be answered promptly and well.

"Don's going to lower my ears and take a little off the top," I reply. A silent giggle passes through the room.

"This is no time for jokes," Nurse fires back. Her voice ratchets up. "These are important questions."

"Yes, ma'am, they are," I reply quietly. "I feel kinda bad about kidding around. You want to provide great care and I'm not making that any easier. I'm here this morning for a transurethral resection of a two-centimeter right-wall papillary tumor."

Nurse blinks, makes a note in her chart, and retreats.

"Things have been tough at home for her lately," another nurse says, patting my arm reassuringly. "She means well, and she's quite good at her job."

"That's what matters," I reply. "Now. Can I also leave with mutton chop sideburns? I've got this tryout next week for the new Elvis show."

Don's head pokes in through the curtains. "Ready to go?" he asks cheerfully.

"Ready or not," I tell him.

"I'll go make sure things are set up," he says. "Mary will be back to get you in a few minutes."

I give Julie's hand a squeeze. She kisses my head and leaves. Alone in my stall, I decide to measure how anxious I am on a scale of zero to 100. I'm surprised to find my number is zero. No anxiety whatsoever. Instead— gratitude. To be lying on this gurney in this place. For having the best surgical team on the planet. For knowing, in my bones, I'm completely ok.

I'll think back on this moment days from now. Realize how wise it is. These could be the final minutes of my life. I'd so prefer to spend them in a state of gratitude than one of fear. To be kidding around with Larry and John. Hearing about others' adventures on roadtrips through the American Southwest. When my last minutes, incoming even now, do arrive, I intend to spend them in precisely this way.

*

Mary arrives with another tech. I'm surprised to see Big Nurse again. Her face and tone are different now. Softer. Warmer.

"Any other questions?" she asks, touching my right foot.

"Thank you," I say. "I appreciate your asking. No questions whatsoever. Y'all do wonderful work."

Mary lowers the gurney's backrest, laying me flat. Fluorescent lights and green ceiling tiles slide by overhead. The double doors to the operating room open and chilly air blows over me. Transferred to the operating table, I stare into the surgical lighthead. *You again?* it seems to say. A tech sticks electrodes across my torso. I glance at the green EKG screen. Other monitors I don't recognize. A mask goes over my nose and mouth, and the oxygen starts flowing. Don's face, smiling behind his surgical mask. Larry's asking if I'm ready to go under. The metallic scent of nitrous oxide and whatever else Larry put in today's soup. He told me the names, but I seem to have forgotten them. I seem...

*

"Welcome back!" a cheerful voice says. "You're all done. Dr. Lamm says things went very well."

A large black bug trundles across the foot of the sheet draped over me. Odd. A big bug here in post-op. After making the considerable effort it takes to focus my eyes, I realize the bug is the tip of my big toe.

Coming out of general anesthesia is like this. It even has a name: postoperative delirium. It can stick around awhile. We'll stop at a pharmacy on the way home. While Julie goes inside, I'll sit in the car and see another shopper exit his car, walk straight through the store's exterior brick wall. Odd: most people use the glass door. Only when the man reappears on the other side of the brick column carrying the portico fronting the store do I realize what actually happened.

The nurse, Cathy, goes to get Julie. Later Julie tells me Cathy advised, "Don't take him too seriously just yet. He was saying all kinds of things when he first woke up."

In Mom's final days in hospice, she had the family laughing harder than we ever had together. As morphine disinhibited her lifelong primness, avoidance of all things erotic, she spoke openly of men in speedos she'd noticed on the beach with all the gusto of late Mae West. Freud called such eruptions "the return of the repressed." We can, for a while, repress the erotic. We can never escape it.

"Hmmm," I say to Julie. "What was I saying?" I'm considering the probabilities that Daniel, apple of Mom's eye, might not have fallen far from the tree.

"Cathy didn't tell me."

"Is that a good thing?"

"Probably. Yes."

*

Three days after my initial surgery, I returned to the hospital to have my catheter removed. As surgery compromises the bladder wall, post-op catheterization ensures no pressure builds up in that organ until it has time to heal. Bladders can burst, a scenario as rare as it is terrifying. Don has said it's nothing we want to traffic in.

POUR is the deadpan acronym for a more common post-op complication: put bluntly, an *inability* to pour. *Postoperative urinary retention* can result from a combination of lingering anesthesia effects, pain meds, and tissue damage to the plumbing involved in normal pouring. My providers all have cautioned that I might have trouble peeing once my catheter is removed. If this happens, I'm to call their office immediately, or head to the nearest ER. Bladder pressure at this point is nobody's friend. All of which lends a certain dramatic tension to first uncatheterized post-op visits to the bathroom.

I've learned to remove my own catheters. Understanding the plumbing involved (my own and the catheter's) is a first step. A long silicone tube drains the bladder into the bag I wear at my hip. Immediately after surgery, Don injected sterile water into a separate channel in the tube, inflating a balloon in the top of the line that prevents it from slipping back out of my bladder. Removal involves 1] standing under a warm shower and disconnecting the tube from the collection bag; 2] using scissors to cut the cap off the balloon port, allowing the sterile water to drain and balloon deflate; 3] tugging lightly on the silicone line until I feel it slither down of its own accord to the floor of the shower. *Ah! That's better!*

Three hours later, I feel an urge to pee. Standing at the urinal in the café's bathroom, I feel the moment's drama build. Here I am, poised and ready to pour. Nothing immediately happens. Then, like some long-forgotten skill, I feel interior and exterior sphincters relax and the golden train come rolling down the tracks. *Ah! Better still!*

I zip up, bow gratefully in the mirror—then notice something interesting. Some part of me is reluctant to fully feel grateful. Some other kind of retention is going on. *Hmmm. What's up with that?*

Over the course of our cancer careers, many of us get pretty good at being grateful for bad news. Recurrences. *We caught it early!* Metastasis. *It only went to the bone!* This is an essential cancer skill. I don't know how we'd live and die well without it.

"I'm an old woman," a leukemia patient told me quietly as she lay dying. Meaning, *I've had my turn. It's been a good run. Now it's time for me to stand down.*

What I hadn't noticed till finishing up at the urinal this morning was the experience of security that comes with readiness to feel gratitude for bad news. I know how to receive it. And when I'm ok with the worst, I'm pretty solid. So far so good. Except now I'm the recipient of good news. I'm again outpouring as I'm designed to do. *How are you now, Daniel?*

Well, I'm somewhat *reluctant*. And curious about this. Talking it out with Julie, I realize another aspect of vulnerability. It seems that, all unawares (as is my wont), I've connected gratitude for good news with *attachment* to good news. Arranged things such that if I'm grateful for good news—for healing, health—I'll be setting myself up for suffering should I again lose these things. The Upanishads noted this dilemma millennia ago. Clinging to anything—bad or good—produces suffering. On some level, we all know anything we cling to can and will be taken from us.

Seeing what I've been up to, I decide to reset. To feel any and all emotions that travel with tidings that come my way. To willingly ride that rollercoaster. No attachment required. Just gratitude for the gift that is the ride.

Cutthroat trout in the Pecos understand this. Protected creatures, they swim in state-designated *red chile water*. If caught, they are released back into the stream from which they were taken. Caught, their whole universe gets turned on its head. Released, they discover themselves back where they belong.

Caught two weeks ago, I'm again released. Don gives his blessing to my return home after I've once peed under my own power. Releasing that first stream releases me into the second: the muscular current of living-cum-dying in which, like the cutthroat, I freely move and breathe and find my way.

Death

Death is the greatest pleasure.
Kyozan Joshu Sasaki

I just wish it were over," my older sister says softly. She's standing behind me in the hospital room with my brother Fred and our other sisters. I'm sitting on a chair next to Dad as he sleeps, my hand resting on his heart. Dad is a terminal Alzheimer's patient. Fourteen years into this disease, his brain and body have all but shut down. He's forgotten his wife of 45 years. Forgotten the names, though not the faces, of his children. Forgotten the real estate company he founded, the prosperity it created.

And now, at age 80, forgotten how to swallow. As saliva pools in the back of his throat, Dad's respiration fills the small room with the sharp death rattle so distressing Nancy.

Hearing her voice, I realize I'm not wishing anything over. Nor wishing anything to continue. Wishing only to be here now, with Dad, just like this. My breathing has synced to his. Together we're riding the rising and falling tidal volume of four lungs, a rhythm that commenced with a gasp for us each decades ago, stopping here and there for two minutes while we swam beside each other underwater the length of Olympic pools. An ebb and flow continuing unabated through the days and nights, connecting us with each other and with all inspiration on the land, in the air, and underwater, the wide clan of lunged creatures. Carrying us forward to this place as the sea decades ago carried us ashore once Dad taught me to clasp my hands beneath my belly and use my body as a surfboard that we might together ride the waves I can hear even now rising and falling not far from this room.

As Dad dozes, I close my eyes and remember others of our adventures. Dad sitting me on his lap in the days before seatbelts to steer the family station wagon home from Sunday Mass. My eyes just peeked over the Buick's metal dashboard, my legs still too short to reach the pedals. Dad showing me how to put my feet through my arms while gripping a high bar, then fall backward, rotating my shoulders 360 degrees. *Shoulder dislocation* Dad called it; I still don't know if that's what happened or not. Coach Dad driving me home in proud silence the evening that my two free throws after the final buzzer tied, then won the game. Dad and I diving off stone cliffs into the Kern River, aiming for the darker green water less likely to have rocks lurking beneath the surface. We might have died— which added an essential ingredient to the experience. *Death defying*, we felt more alive than at most other times.

Now we're on our most extreme adventure to date: dying. Defiance no longer an option. Per usual, Dad is going first. In the last days, his going, this last high dive, has taught me much. As his one-and-one-half pikes off the three-meter board taught me, his backflip off the ten-meter platform. No longer able to speak, Dad sees a new orderly enter the room. Greets the surprised young man with a broad smile, motions to find the newcomer a chair. *Does he believe this another of his children? Does he still make such distinctions?*

This is how I want to die. Entirely focused on those around me. Creating no distinctions. *Have a seat! Please, make yourself at home!*

*

The words living and dying make it difficult to grasp that to which they point. Binary terms appear to denote a dichotomous reality: we're living, or else we're dying. Yet what these words point to is something continuous—a continuum. Every second, in any human body, well or ill, one-half million cells die natural deaths. This makes 300 million deaths per minute, 432 billion deaths—one percent of our physical structure—daily. We're hardwired for precisely this living-cum-dying. It is the foundation of our growth and development and protective against threats posed by immortal cell lines, one of cancer's singular traits. In healthy tissue, all cells live-cum-die. Cancer cells may live (and divide) forever.

Human being, like light, is a wave-particle duality. Adult humans are a collection of 37 trillion individual cells. Over the course of a lifetime, virtually all these cells will be left behind. As a wave crashing onto a beach started out as a single offshore water molecule moving in a new direction, humans, too, start out as single cells. The wave of us builds as it passes through spacetime. Then relinquishes itself on the far shore.

At conception, a cellular birthday candle gets lit. Called a telomere, it's a repetitive nucleotide sequence at the end of each chromosome. Telomeres protect chromosomes—and hence the genetic material they encode—from damage. So here's the thing: with each cellular division, telomeres shorten, making their length a precise measure of the age of a particular cell line. Human cells lose on average 50 base pairs of telomeric DNA each year. Our candles burn down. Dad's telomeres are always shorter than mine, which are always shorter than my son's, which are always shorter than those of his sons. *Happy Birthday!* we sing each lap of the planet around its star. We blow the candles out, as one day the star will go out. This joyous ritual. This memento mori.

What happens if cellular candles stop burning down? Or reverse themselves and start lengthening? Cancer happens. The protein telomerase, which builds telomeres in germ cells, is normally turned off in utero. Cancer hijacks chemical processes in the tissue neighborhood charged with regulating telomerase, reactivating this protein and lengthening telomeres in malignant cells. *Hey-Guys!* now has a blank check to propagate mutant cell lines forever. Or until their host, in Dad's words, *Bites the dust. Kicks the bucket. Checks out.*

*

While all world spiritual paths advise their version of memento mori, remembering or being anywhere near death and dying is not our first impulse. I use the word "our" in its broadest sense: beings as various as lobsters and house finches social distance themselves from sick and dying members of their communities.

I was living in a communal rooming house in downtown Los Angeles when a fellow resident died one night in his room. Our little household included a cat named Mozambique we'd rescued from the streets. Mo's favorite pastime was patrolling the long hallway our rooms gave onto, darting through any open doorway to explore a new interior. Following Freddy's death, we left his door and window open to air the room out. Mo never again ventured inside. He would, in fact, sprint by the open doorway, a behavior we'd never observed before.

One of my patients served multiple tours of duty in Vietnam as an Army Ranger. He led small groups of men on weeks-long reconnaissance missions behind enemy lines. Whenever possible, he slept in a local cemetery. Vietnamese friends told him it was very unlikely that a Vietcong patrol would venture into such places after dark. While behind enemy lines, these were the only nights my patient slept soundly. Slept "the sleep of the dead," he quipped, with that mordant flicker of amusement only combat vets can muster.

In traditional Diné culture, contact with a ch'įįdii—the spirit that rises from a body at death—is believed to cause "ghost sickness," a PTSD-like affliction of body and mind. Contact with a dead person's belongings will also cause ghost sickness, as will inhabiting a structure in which that person died. Diné or Vietnamese, avian or feline, the vertebrate genome seems hardwired to avoid all things death and dying. We could see this hardwiring is *Way-Things's* castle keep, a refuge of first and last resort against the slings and arrows of outrageous fortune.

What feelings of security arise from avoidance of death come with a price tag. When we avoid something—death, needles, flying on airplanes—our brain takes note and files away this data in support of the hypothesis that the avoided thing is Very Bad Indeed. Very Dangerous. As this data accumulates, the approach of that dreaded thing will trigger worry, then anxiety, and finally outright panic and terror.

If the emotional price of avoidance becomes too great, one can reach for a CBT tool called "exposure." Instead of continuing to avoid something, we can walk toward it and check it out for ourselves. What is the reality of that thing we've been avoiding? Not our thoughts about the thing, but the thing itself.

Sāva sadhana is a yogic practice that exposes practitioners very directly to death. It is done at night, by oneself, in a cemetery, cremation ground, or other remote place. The devotee first performs an elaborate ceremony honoring and preparing a new corpse for the ritual. He or she then sits on the corpse and meditates through the night. Sometimes I'll recommend that a patient fearful of death and dying volunteer at a hospice—a contemporary Western version of sāva sadhana. Very often such exposure to the *reality* of dying and death displaces fearful *thinking* about them, liberating patients from their irrational fears.

*

"Because we have the wrong attitude toward living, we have the wrong attitude toward dying," one of my teachers told me. What is our wrong attitude toward living?

I once treated a depressed patient in his seventies. A successful medical professional, a handsome, physically healthy man with plenty of money, his chief complaint was his inability to attract a partner in her forties. Single, he believed he couldn't be happy without such a companion. He got regular Botox injections, worked out at the gym, and cruised venues where he thought he might connect with this woman of his dreams. As unsuccess followed unsuccess, he became suicidal, wondering if death might be preferable to his sad, lonely, bleak existence.

Our wrong attitude toward living always boils down to this: a belief we need something other than the very fact pattern of reality to be happy. Something other than the sharp truth of birth, development, old age, and death. Something other than those facial lines, that puffiness under our eyes. Over time, my patient came to understand that his desire for a younger mate was an immortality project: a younger woman would vicariously connect him with his own younger self. At a mostly subconscious level, he felt such a relationship would be death-defying.

Once he became consciously aware of this project, my patient had a decision to make: carry on with this agenda or settle into the reality of whom and how he was. The reality of a man, as my father (athlete to the end) would say of himself, *in the fourth quarter.*

Another patient, a woman in her fifties with incurable cancer, came to me for help with panic attacks. In our work together, she identified a subconscious belief she'd carried with her since childhood. A belief triggered by her father's sudden death at the age of 40: *Death is a huge mistake!*

Herein lay the root of her panic. When this belief became activated by her cancer diagnosis, it unleashed a cascade of panicky thoughts. *OMG! Not me! I haven't yet done what I was born to do!* An existential mistake, an error in being, is huge indeed; it pulls the carpet out from under everything else.

I helped this patient evaluate, then reject this lifelong belief. She decided that though as a healthy person it might have helped her, as a cancer patient it was no help at all. She decided to accept the reality of her and others' deaths, to see it not as a mistake but as a natural, necessary part of the big (and good) picture of living-cum-dying. Resetting this core belief marked the beginning of the end of her terror. She was now able and willing to relax into the reality of her mortality, into her true nature.

Relax into. Here we have the *right* attitude toward living. Relaxed into living, so, too, may we relax into dying. The alternative is never pretty. Botox at 70 is far more than a neurotoxin.

*

Dad had been teaching me about dying for much of his fourth quarter. Alzheimer's first and last death is that of memory. Dad's gradual demise presented a slow-motion clip of this loss. Before ever being diagnosed, he'd complain about losing track of everyday objects: keys, wallet, letters to be mailed. I'd see lengthening lists of reminders written in his scribbled longhand on the yellow legal pad on his desk.

"I don't like thinking about where this all might lead," he'd say.

Then came diagnosis, followed by a cascade of more overt losses. The faces and names of family. The ability to recite the Rosary, to walk into his neighborhood of many years and certainly find his way home. Cognizance of the need to shower, shave, or brush his teeth. This once supremely capable man regressed to the mental capacity of one of his young great-grandsons.

With notable exceptions. Even in his last days, Dad could look at a picture in his college yearbook and name all his football teammates and the positions they played. Dad could still throw a football in a perfect spiral in our games of catch at the beach. When he was finally too weak to stand, I bought a Nerf football and, at the foot of his bed, we'd reenact pass plays he'd drilled me in half a century before.

"Ok Dad," I'd say. "I'm going down and out to the right."

Dad would nod, lick the fingertips of his passing hand, find the laces on the ball, and let fly. As he weakened, his passes fell increasingly short, landing not in my hands but in the covers at the foot of the bed. When they did, the same disappointment crossed his face as I imagined crossed it in his college days well before I was born.

As Dad lost much of his past, I realized for the first time how shared memory is the foundation stone for relationship. It's what distinguishes a loved one from any stranger on a bus. I learned to stop asking Dad what I realized was a perennial question for both my folks: *Remember when...?* The answer was always no—followed by awkward, sad silence on both sides. I learned instead to default to playing catch, getting ice cream cones, sitting on a bench at the beach watching the surfers and the shore birds. These moments live on in me today. Are among my favorite mementos of Dad in the slowly fading gallery of my own, of all memory.

*

Dad died during Lent, the Catholic season commemorating the death of Jesus. In his last days, we kids sang him songs he'd taught us as children, showed him pictures of his grandchildren, read him passages from his well-thumbed prayer book. One such passage, taken from John's Gospel, renders dying Jesus's cry: τετέλεσται. English translations include, *It is consummated. It is complete. It is perfect.* As a marriage is consummated, made perfect, completed in the act of love.

We could hear Jesus's last cry as his death poem. Such poems arose in the Zen tradition, principally in Japan. They are a final, often exuberant exclamation marking this vital moment. In this spirit, the *It* marked by τετέλεσται could be seen as living-cum-dying. This moment, exactly like all moments, is perfect. Complete. Existence is completion itself. The kingdom of God lies within it. Apart from our living-cum-dying, there is no kingdom. Realizing this fact, like Jesus we enter the kingdom. Not realizing this fact, we remain eternally outside the gates.

At the end, Jesus and Lao Tzu speak with one voice: in each moment there is never anything left undone.

*

As Dad brought the right attitude to living, he brought the right attitude toward dying. Dying well, he completed an arc that began with his birth—to a mother who would always love him right down to the ground. To a father who left his family forever as soon as his wife became pregnant with her only child. Really to grasp any life, you need to follow its contour from beginning to end. Really to understand a river, you need to travel from its headwaters to the estuary where it returns to the sea. Following the river of Dad's birth, life and death I understand its magnificent shape. Its interdependence with the arc of my own existence. Without a father, there is no son. Without a son, no father. We are born into these ties that bind. We die into them as well.

"Death is the mother of beauty," Wallace Stevens wrote. A sunset, a cherry blossom, a parent that lives forever would not be beautiful. Would be, in fact, monstrous, appalling. Dad, me, my son are the beautiful progeny of this, our first mother. Only because we are forever slipping through each other's fingers do we touch each other's hearts.

*

Here's good news: the right attitude is contagious.

My sister Kathy was diagnosed with multiple sclerosis seven years before Dad's death. Like Alzheimer's disease, MS disrupts electrical transmission in the central nervous system. Both diseases are characterized by plaques in the brain. For the first seven years of her illness, Kathy told me she was grateful to live in a state where medical aid in dying is sanctioned. When she determined that her care was becoming too great a burden on her loved ones, she could end her life on her own terms.

"Makes sense to me," I told her. "Just make sure you call me so I can be with you when you drink that Kool-Aid." A few months after Dad's death, the topic came back up between us.

"I've rethought the Kool-Aid thing," Kathy told me.

"How so?" I asked.

"Seeing the gift Dad gave us by dying," she replied, "I realized I don't want to deny my own family that gift. So y'all are now stuck with me—for the duration."

*

And yet, and yet...

I read in the local paper of the death of a friend and neighbor and fellow cancer patient. Julia was a woman about my age, an artist, alternative healer, and wonderfully light and gentle soul. In a time of pandemic—and with our compromised immune systems—we'd not seen each other for over a year. Our paths last crossed in the bulk food section of the local market ten days before I read her obituary. I was happy, as always, to see her. And felt torn. Part of me wanted to hug her and catch up on things. Another wanted to maintain our social distance, finish shopping, and get out of the crowded store. I imagine she might have felt torn as well. Now she was gone.

"I can't believe it!" I tell Julie, denial always my first line of defense. "I just saw her at the market!"

As if this sighting conferred rights to Julia's presence. As if coparticipation in ordinary human life somehow guarantees its duration. Reading Julia's obituary, I felt a pang of remorse at our truncated last meeting. Had I any inkling these were our last minutes together, I would have lingered, thanked Julia for the gift of herself, wept with her there next to the bulk organic granola.

"In a world without heaven to follow," Stevens wrote, "the stops would be endings, more poignant than partings, profounder...

*

Mom and Dad called the open ocean their "blue desert." They named their sailboat Pilgrimage. Crossing the shipping lanes, they took turns keeping watch through the night, as the Gospel of Luke reports the shepherds had done. Mom and Dad both described these solitary vigils as among the best moments of their voyages.

Like countless pilgrims before them, my folks traveled into the desert to meet God. Reading their ship's log down through the years, I concluded they succeeded. Here is Mom's entry at 11:30 p.m. on July 22. Latitude 42° N, Longitude 149° W. In lay terms, the middle of the Pacific Ocean in the middle of the night:

Saw a freighter due north of us. In 30 minutes it disappeared over the horizon. Such a black night! Like sailing in a bowl of black ink. No earth, sea or sky. Just blackness all around me. Must be like this leaving the earth through the black door of death. A most peaceful feeling. God is very close.

This is the one mention I know that Mom ever made of dying. In acute care at the hospital, two weeks before her death, Mom asked Dad to take her home, against all medical advice. Dad, her quarterback, father of her children, her first and last mate, looked at her a long moment.

"Do you know what you're asking?"

"I do," Mom replied.

"Then we're going home," he said.

Only later did I realize this is what Mom said when she'd married Dad 43 years earlier. *I do. Till death do us part.*

*

In her last week, Mom was in and out of a coma, sailing ever deeper into that blackness she'd foreseen. Now it was we her children keeping watch, by day and by night, the hours threaded like rosary beads on something that felt equally temporal and timeless. We took turns moistening Mom's lips with ice chips, placing cold washcloths on her forehead, cleaning her when she soiled herself, hitting the morphine pump if she appeared in too much pain.

Just after midnight on Saturday morning, my brother Fred took up watch beside her. Mom opened her eyes, looked directly at him, and smiled. She weakly raised her left hand, waved farewell to her firstborn child, and died.

Fred woke the rest of us and we physically gathered as family one last time. I sat on a pillow on Mom's bed, in the cross-legged position I assume each morning to pray. I placed my hand on her still-warm skin. I wanted Mom and I, together, to fix this final position: 33° N, 117° W. After all our wide voyaging, *bon & mal*, together and apart, over land and sea and through the air, we'd arrived but 53 land miles south of 33° N, 117° W, where, 39 years earlier, Dr. Slater handed Mom her April Fool. Our final reckoning placed us 679 nautical miles north of where, tomorrow at noon, the sun would stand directly over the Tropic of Cancer.

*

I needed Mom's help charting my new course into this *mare incognitum,* unknown sea of life as a motherless child. Settling in together this first morning, I'm astonished at how natural everything feels. *Like childbirth,* I think. Very *ordinary*—from the Latin: "of the order of things." Living well, Mom died well. Like Ignatius. The future saint's faithful secretary, Juan Alfonso de Polanco, sat at Ignatius's bedside throughout his last days and nights. Upon his friend's death, Polanco wrote, "He departed this world in the most ordinary way."

Next, I'm astonished to discover something more: that there's no such *thing* as death. I'd assumed that word, a noun, pointed to some entity, as the word *star* points to fire, the word *compass* to the magnetometer in the helm of a sailboat. And pointed to a thing to be dreaded most of all. Dreaded more than I dreaded, despite Mom's assurances, the nighttime monster beneath my boyhood bed. Yet here, in the early morning darkness, there is no entity, no thing. We've been afraid of death for so long. When there is, quite literally, no thing to fear.

*

So—what is there?

Sitting with Mom this morning—and each morning since—I sit in the depths of a sea older than the super-ocean Panthalassa. Mom rose, a wave in that sea, in 1930 in Chicago, Illinois, 41° N, 87° W. She returned to its depths in Dana Point, California, in 1995. Because she rose, I rose. My son and grandsons rose. Each of us are following the arc of Mom's return to these depths. In the sounds of Mom's laughter and my son's and his sons' and their sons' I hope one day to hear, deep calls unto deep. This is family. These are the ties that bind. Bind the Mintie clan. And bind together all beings past, present, and future. Never, for a single instant, are we separate. Never are we apart.

God is very close.

*

A few nights later, I have a dream:

I'm lying newly dead on a white cotton winding-sheet. A small group of people attend me. They wrap the shroud round my body, then pick me up and carry me on a path that circles and ascends a high mountain. For three days and three nights they carry me, three times around the mountain. We arrive just before sunrise at the summit. I'm placed on my feet and the cloth is unwound. I open my eyes just as the sun appears and realize my body is now weightless, filled with and the same as this great light. The whole of brightening heaven, the whole earth is not other than my own body.

I wake from the dream into the same weightless-ness, one now with the darkness of the room in which I've lain sleeping.

"Ah," I say aloud. "So this is how it is."

Priority

There was a muddy centre before we breathed.
There was a myth before the myth began,
Venerable and articulate and complete.
Wallace Stevens

Pecos Wilderness, the fall equinox. Two days ago, Julie and I hoisted room and board on our backs and packed 10,000 feet up into the dry September air. This morning, yellow warblers, round as lemons, flit amongst the aspen branches, whistling through the day's upper register. Nights the Northern Cross rises with the Milky Way. Meteors drop from the apex into the jagged black tree line atop the gneiss cliff behind us.

Returning to the wild, we always experience a day or two of psychological withdrawal. Humans are a wild species, yet our ways domesticate us. It's wrenching, at first, to trade electricity, fossil fuel, *the news cycle*, for simple, timeless acts like drawing water, gathering wood. Then it becomes a huge relief.

Back in the Pecos, we begin to reexperience priority, the place from which the rest of life emerges. A locus Hermes Trismegistus called "a circle whose center is everywhere, whose circumference is nowhere." Reexperience what's essential. Doing so, we remember that what lies directly at hand is always enough. We have an entire high meadow to ourselves. A river runs through it. Trees provide shade at midday and heat after sundown. Living so simply and so well, I ask a question my parents asked after weeks aboard Pilgrimage in their blue desert. *Why do we have that big house? Why all the gadgets?*

As our days grow simpler, so do our minds. We talk less, perhaps because we think less. Thinking doesn't add much value here. When it does arise, it feels recreational—like napping in the afternoon shade or plunging into the glacial stream, to the astonishment of its icy denizens. After three days, I jot these notes on a pad of paper I packed along just in case. Writing the first letters feels like constructing hieroglyphs. Making sense of my first sentences involves unusual effort, like reading lines in German or Spanish.

Recreation. From the Latin noun *recreationem*: "recovery from illness." What illness? Too much thinking. Or better: too much attention paid to thinking. Cognition and language are miraculous tools. Wise guys evolved a neocortex specifically to traffic in these ephemera. Yet most of us seem less likely to *use* these tools than to be used *by* thought. Less likely to engage reality than to engage, all higgledy-piggledy, thoughts about reality.

In his poem "Holiday in Reality," Wallace Stevens writes of such recreation, such recovery: *The flowering Judas grows from the belly or not at all... Spring is umbilical or else it is not spring.* Seasons are rooted in, emerge from the gut, not the head. Heady seasons are fake seasons, distractions, wastes of life force.

*

Solitary night watches onboard Pilgrimage, steeped in silence amongst the stars, were among my folks' favorite times on the blue water. In monasteries, Vigils is the first monastic hour of communal prayer each day. It begins at four, well before first light. I notice this is when Julie gets up each morning, crawling through the tent flap and meditating for two hours beneath those same stars. I follow her at sunrise to do the same.

My parents' boy, I love prayer. As a child, I memorized Our Father and Hail Mary and a few other scripted pleas. As a teenager, I abandoned these words, though I continued praying *to* or *for* someone or something. Put differently, I still experienced myself as separate from God. Prayer became longing across the divide of that separation. Longing for that divine union John of the Cross and mystics of every tradition describe.

Longing. Now *there's* the rub! Real happiness, real freedom, comes not from getting what we want. Nor from everywhere and always doing what we want. This is actually the first form of captivity: life at the behest of a tyrant. Living at the whim of a despot whose claim to absolute power is illegitimate. Happiness, real freedom, is life lived *a priori*, in the great wide open. Life beholden to the fact pattern of the universe, the interdependent co-arising occurring all around. The soil. Water. The request of a family member.

When we begin spiritual practice, we think of divine union as the ego's acquisition of something called God. As we deepen our prayer, we realize union comes with the *dissolution* of egoity, the renunciation of any and all acquisition. As spiritual children, we think of heaven as a place where the ego can kick back and enjoy itself for all eternity.

In fact, there is such a place. It's called hell.

*

Pecos mornings I'm content simply to pray. Let prayer itself do the praying. No need any longer for *one who prays* separate from the rest of the universe. I pray as the river prays, unselfconsciously, its happy coincidence of hydrogen, oxygen, and gravity falling through the wider animal, vegetable, and mineral kingdoms, filling the meadow with a sound like the applause of a midsize audience, brought to its feet by something done just right. True applause: not *to* or *for* anything. Applause that is, like prayer, but the cry of its occasion. *Venerable, articulate, and complete.*

*

The Japanese Zen master Eihei Dōgen writes, "Mountains, rivers, Earth, the Sun, the Moon, the stars *are* mind." These entities surrounding us comprise the structure of reality, known in Chinese as *xin*. *Xin* is translated as *heart*, as *mind*, or as both: *heart/mind*. We *are* these gneiss cliffs, this sparkling river, this cathedral of gold aspen leaves, this boundless sky. Precisely as it's impossible to stand outside our own bodies and take them in, it's impossible to stand outside and grasp *xin*. Why? Because there is no outside.

All world paths speak to *xin*, our prior condition. The King James Bible relates that Adam and Eve, living in Eden, *were naked... and were not ashamed.* The Sumerian word from which Eden derives translates as *uncultivated. Natural.* Living in Eden, we embody our natural condition. We eat when we're hungry. Sleep when we're tired. We are nakedly, unashamedly, simply ourselves. We have nothing to cover over, nothing to cover up. The Genesis story states a deep truth, less about first ancestors than about ourselves. You and I are Adam and Eve. We are always, already, living in and as this natural state.

The Genesis story continues: *And the LORD God commanded the man, saying, Of every tree of the garden thou may freely eat: But of the tree of the knowledge of good and evil, thou shalt not eat: for on the day thou eat thereof, thou shalt surely die.* God, like Gregory Wertz, is right, of course. As soon as we label something, we separate ourselves from our natural state. We won't find labels in nature, in the Garden. Making and wholeheartedly buying into such judgments removes us from our naturalness, casts us out of Eden.

Evil. Good. Malignant. Benign.

*

I walk into Don's waiting room and join two patients a bit older than me. Early in my cancer career, I learned silence in an oncologist's waiting room is nobody's friend. If we're not actively engaged with each other, we're engaged in worried thought. Taking the mind path through these minutes or—should Don run into something unforeseen—hours. The mind path, under such conditions, is not a scenic route. So I've made a habit of striking up conversation. Speaking encouraging words to a frightened new patient. Swapping war stories with other grizzled veterans.

"Just another day in paradise," a guy in an army cap growls by way of greeting.

"That's how I see it," I tell him. The other guy looks up at me and grins.

Niceties done, we talk turkey. Neil tells me of his first surgery with a different oncologist. The lack of any meaningful aftercare. His crowbarring his way in to see Don, who did a cysto and found thirty tumors in Neil's bladder.

"Thirty!" Neil says, shaking his head in disbelief these decades later. "That was eight surgeries ago. Now the cancer is trying to move up into my left kidney. Don placed a port just beneath it, is putting BCG directly into the ureter. I think he really wants to save that kidney. Me too! If I lose it, I'll have to start dialysis, which I don't want to do. I mean, I would, of course. Any morning you wake with a pulse is a good morning."

As we talk, I realize Neil is not making judgments. Things aren't good or bad. Things are just themselves. *Thirty tumors!* Neil is living in Eden, in his natural condition. He's figured out how to be a successful cancer patient. Thus figured out how to live-cum-die. Which is the reason he clearly sees the truth that lies at the end of every spiritual path: any morning with a pulse is a good morning. Another day in paradise.

*

"Hike to the beaver dam?" Julie asks.

"Love to," I tell her. We lace on our boots and start up the trail.

The dam is one of the Pecos wonders. One hundred yards long, it dwarfs a single beaver the way Egypt's pyramids dwarf a single Egyptian. Ten generations of animals built it—without plans, without tools, without language. Today their masterwork blesses the valley as much as it blesses the pelted clan *Castor canadensis*. It filters the river's water, reducing sediment. Slows streamflow, thereby decreasing erosion. Builds riparian wetlands, habitat for many other marsh critters. Cutthroat beneath the dam, gorging on its macronutrients, grow fatter than cutthroat in any other section of the river.

Without plan, without language. With what then?

With *genius loci*, as it was called in classical Rome. The *genius of the place*. In one of his poems, Alexander Pope advises:

> *Consult the genius of the place in all;*
> *That tells the waters to rise, or fall;*
> *Or helps th' ambitious hill the heav'ns to scale;*
> *Or scoops in circling theatres the vale...*

Eden knows its way. Prior to thought, prior to language, prior to making judgments or plans. Unselfconsciously. Humans speak of conscience. Which, rather than *knowledge of good and evil*, we might better understand as *genius loci*. The word *conscience* comes to us from Latin roots that denote *knowing* and *together*. The word points to that which, prior to thinking, we all *know*. As the beaver, unthinkingly, knows. *Xin*. How to live, what to do.

*

I step off the trail to pee, my sudden yellow arc sparkling in sunlight sifting through the spruce branches. Twenty-nine seasons ago, along this same trail, I first glimpsed hematuria. First saw red at the solstice. Today's only crimson is the occasional flash of a cutthroat lashing to the river's surface to feed.

Vast resources made possible my standing here this morning. Hundreds of hours of highly skilled care by dozens of providers. Advanced medicines and cutting-edge medical equipage. Twenty-nine seasons of Julie's attention and care and that of so many family members, patients, colleagues, and friends. All this outlay resting atop the enormous consumption that makes US citizens' carbon footprints five times the global average. At my last visit, Don told me, great sadness in his eyes, of another effect of the ongoing shortage of BCG in the global supply chain: a 1,000% increase in childhood mortality (due to tuberculosis) in the Third World. I did the brutally simple math: each dose going into my bladder goes not into the arm of one of these children.

"To whom much is given, much will be required," Jesus tells us in Luke's Gospel. Standing in Pecos's aromatic fall air, I ask myself, *What is required of me?* Per Catechism Question 145: *In light of these truths, what should you do?*

One answer: *Write a book.*

*

Living-cum-dying. So then, prior to birth and death: what about that?

This question lies at the bottom of all philosophy, religion, and spiritual practice. Directly seeing into this first and last reality is what, finally, frees us from all conditions, all dichotomies. Please be clear: directly seeing doesn't *spare* us any condition. Conditions, illness and health for instance, comprise our existence the way seasons comprise our climate. Directly seeing only frees us from being *bound* by conditions, being limited or defined by them. Directly seeing, we realize all such conditions are themselves perfect expressions of that prior ground sometimes called *absolute reality*. Sometimes called *God*. Condition and ground are warp and woof of our living-cum-dying. No condition is a fundamental problem. Cancer included. Hospice included. Any condition is a fundamental opportunity. Fundamental gift. Is, in fact, our only opportunity. Only gift.

The Prajñāpāramitāhṛdaya, a Sanskrit poem that sets forth the heart of Buddhist teaching, puts it this way: *There is no old age, sickness or death. Also no ending of old age, sickness and death.*

When the disciple Phillip asked Jesus to show him the Father, Jesus answered "Anyone who has seen me has seen the Father."

One of my Zen teachers describes the warp and woof of existence in mathematic terms. "It's like a fraction," he told me. "The numerator is the individual, the denominator absolute reality. The fraction, be it a human being or anything else, cannot exist without both sides."

This teacher once asked his own teacher about human death. His teacher, an old man at the time, sat quietly for awhile. He then replied softly "There's always the numerator."

*

Pecos night. *Bowl of black ink.* Smoke from our campfire drifting into the stars. The river running louder than it does in daylight. A sudden rustle in the dry grasses behind us. Call of a solitary night bird arriving on the spruce-infused air.

Julie sits on the ground between my legs, leaning against my chest. My arms around her, our fingers interlaced against the cold, we watch shapes at play in the flames. Human figures. Animals. Mythic creatures. A red metal truck I played with as a boy. Watching long enough, we'd see every form in the world appear there. Glancing back toward the rustle in the understory, I see our shadows dancing on the trunks behind us.

Plato gave us the allegory of a cave: prisoners chained in a cavern facing its back wall. A fire behind them casting shadows on the wall. The prisoners mistaking these projections for the whole of reality. A shadow show the only universe they know.

Many of us much of the time live prisoners' lives. Day and night, electromagnetic impulses in our frontal lobes travel from neuron to neuron, functions of changes in electrical charge within and around each cell. Put differently—we *think*. And thinking is quite like shadows playing on the back wall of a cave. This is human nature, this theater the end result of an evolutionary process that began in the superocean Panthalassa. Thinking is something we're designed to do.

It's what happens next that imprisons us: mistaking this theater for reality itself. Mistaking our *thoughts about* existence for existence itself. Now, like Plato's prisoners, we live out our days in a make-believe of our own conjuring. The wide world becomes but a screen on which we project the show. Attending more to our projections than to the screen, living-cum-dying goes missing.

Julie turns her face to mine, kisses my cheek. "I love you," she says.

*

Julie and I have gotten closer over the course of our cancer career. From my side, I'd say the disease has taken me down a notch. Made me more available to her. More human. Something like this happens for many couples, and it has medical implications. A colleague's research suggests a loving bond is significantly predictive of cancer patients' survival. Cancer has a way of showing us who we really are, as individuals and couples. We reach down together and find what we find.

Cancer sometimes breaks relationships, as does the death of a child. Here too we might say it clarifies who we've been all along.

Along the cancer road I've come more clearly to see how much of what passes for relational life embodies the prisoners' error. We relate less to the reality of each other than to our ideas about that reality. Relationship becomes like the paper dolls my sisters played with growing up. We hold up images of ourselves, cardboard cutouts we dress in various guises. Others do the same. Now relationship becomes a game of paper dolls, the ones holding the dolls seldom appearing at all.

Why would we do this?

Paper-doll relationships seem to arise from another fundamental mistake: failing to recognize that, prior to all our posing, we're already intimate with each other. Which is another way of saying we're already deeply in love. Jesus often points to this fact. So does Buddha, Lao Tzu, and the rest of the gang. The trouble starts when we miss this first reality and start editing ourselves and others in attempts to *make* each other lovable. Out come the scissors, the outfits, the folding tabs.

In other words, the trouble starts with our humanness. And, right here start our possibilities.

*

Committed relationships are intimacy's first proving grounds. If we're well connected with our families, the door opens for authentic connection with the rest of the world. If we're not living in authentic connection with the folks at home, that door to wider connection tends to remain shut. I don't entirely understand why this is so but some others see it this way as well.

"The entire problem of human suffering starts like this," a teacher once told me. "Our spouse calls us from another room and we answer, "Sorry, hon. I'm busy right now."

Practicing any response, we perfect it. And what we perfect is what will come up—when cancer comes calling. When death comes calling.

The call of a spouse, like that of a towhee, calls us to attention when we're lost in ourselves. Calls us home.

*

We might view egoity—living-cum-dying in our mental projections—as an activity separate from and opposed to reality. Separate from and opposed to our *original nature. God.* This indeed appears to be the case. We could rightly view our dreams while sleeping as absorption in unreality. None of our nighttime monsters or fairy godmothers have ever been met in the daytime world.

In another way, such thinking falls into its own trap. Egoity is as much an expression of absolute reality as anything else. God needs egoity to realize herself. Egoity is God's paper doll game. God's playing hide-and-seek with himself. Quite like when my young grandson places his hands over his face and I wonder aloud, "Hey! Where did Brody go?"

Egoity is God's placing God's hands over God's face.

*

Our fire slowly burns down to embers—red and blue and gold mementos of itself. The firepit stones still radiate warmth, even as night's chill slips like a blade beneath our clothing. We linger awhile, alone and together, *dozing in the depths of wakefulness,* here now and most anywhere in spacetime, awash in the rising sound of the black river, the original blessing now.

ABOUT THE AUTHOR

Daniel Mintie is a cognitive-behavioral therapist, teacher, and writer based in Taos, New Mexico, USA. He teaches cognitive-behavioral therapy at universities and training centers worldwide, including: Georgetown University in Washington, DC; the University of New Mexico; the Feeling Good Institute in Mountain View, California; the National Institute for Mental Health and Neuroscience in Bangalore, India; Mexico City's Universidad Hebraica; and the Zentrum fur Psychotherapie in Stuttgart, Germany. He is the author of two previous books: *Reclaiming Life After Trauma* (Healing Arts Press, 2018) and *Dharma Wheels: Zen, Motorcycling & Cognitive-Behavioral Therapy* (Livingwell Publishing, 2020).

Made in the USA
Monee, IL
02 September 2021

77144140R00079